The U.S.
Attack on
Afghanistan

Other books in the At Issue in History series:

The U.S. Attack on Afghanistan

John Boaz, *Book Editor*

Bruce Glassman, *Vice President*
Bonnie Szumski, *Publisher*
Helen Cothran, *Managing Editor*
Scott Barbour, *Series Editor*

 OPPOSING VIEWPOINTS® SERIES AT ISSUE IN HISTORY

GREENHAVEN PRESS
An imprint of Thomson Gale, a part of The Thomson Corporation

 **THOMSON**
™
GALE

Detroit • New York • San Francisco • San Diego • New Haven, Conn.
Waterville, Maine • London • Munich

958.104
USA

For more information, contact
Greenhaven Press
27500 Drake Rd.
Farmington Hills, MI 48331-3535
Or you can visit our Internet site at http://www.gale.com

LIBRARY OF CONGRESS CATALOGING-IN-PUBLICATION DATA

The U.S. attack on Afghanistan / John Boaz, book editor.
    p. cm. — (At issue in history)
Includes bibliographical references and index.
ISBN 0-7377-1983-4 (lib. : alk. paper)
    1. Afghan War, 2001—United States. 2. Afghanistan—History—2001– .
3. United States—Relations—Afghanistan. 4. Afghanistan—Relations—United States. I. Title: US attack on Afghanistan. II. Title: United States attack on Afghanistan. III. Boaz, John. IV. Series.
DS371.412.U14 2005
958.104'6—dc22   2004061689

Contents

Chapter 3: U.S. Involvement in Reconstructing Afghanistan

Foreword

Historian Robert Weiss defines history simply as "a record and interpretation of past events." Both elements—record and interpretation—are necessary, Weiss argues.

> Names, dates, places, and events are the essence of history. But historical writing is not a compendium of facts. It consists of facts placed in a sequence to tell a connected story. A work of history is not merely a story, however. It also must analyze what happened and *why*—that is, it must interpret the past for the reader.

For example, the events of December 7, 1941, that led President Franklin D. Roosevelt to call it "a date which will live in infamy" are fairly well known and straightforward. A force of Japanese planes and submarines launched a torpedo and bombing attack on American military targets in Pearl Harbor, Hawaii. The surprise assault sank five battleships, disabled or sank fourteen additional ships, and left almost twenty-four hundred American soldiers and sailors dead. On the following day, the United States formally entered World War II when Congress declared war on Japan.

These facts and consequences were almost immediately communicated to the American people who heard reports about Pearl Harbor and President Roosevelt's response on the radio. All realized that this was an important and pivotal event in American and world history. Yet the news from Pearl Harbor raised many unanswered questions. Why did Japan decide to launch such an offensive? Why were the attackers so successful in catching America by surprise? What did the attack reveal about the two nations, their people, and their leadership? What were its causes, and what were its effects? Political leaders, academic historians, and students look to learn the basic facts of historical events and to read the intepretations of these events by many different sources, both primary and secondary, in order to develop a more complete picture of the event in a historical context.

In the case of Pearl Harbor, several important questions surrounding the event remain in dispute, most notably the role of President Roosevelt. Some historians have blamed his policies for deliberately provoking Japan to attack in order to propel America into World War II; a few have gone so far as to accuse him of knowing of the impending attack but not informing others. Other historians, examining the same event, have exonerated the president of such charges, arguing that the historical evidence does not support such a theory.

The Greenhaven At Issue in History series recognizes that many important historical events have been interpreted differently and in some cases remain shrouded in controversy. Each volume features a collection of articles that focus on a topic that has sparked controversy among eyewitnesses, contemporary observers, and historians. An introductory essay sets the stage for each topic by presenting background and context. Several chapters then examine different facets of the subject at hand with readings chosen for their diversity of opinion. Each selection is preceded by a summary of the author's main points and conclusions. A bibliography is included for those students interested in pursuing further research. An annotated table of contents and thorough index help readers to quickly locate material of interest. Taken together, the contents of each of the volumes in the Greenhaven At Issue in History series will help students become more discriminating and thoughtful readers of history.

Introduction

United States warplanes attacked radar facilities in
Afghanistan on the evening of October 7, 2001, in an
effort to destroy the military capabilities of Afghanistan's
ruling regime, the Islamic fundamentalist Taliban government. The Taliban harbored the al Qaeda terrorist network
and its leader, Osama bin Laden, who was thought to be the
mastermind behind the attacks on New York and Washington, D.C., on September 11, 2001. When the Taliban failed
to hand bin Laden over to Western authorities, a U.S.-led
coalition launched Operation Enduring Freedom, a military
campaign with the goal of removing the Taliban from
power and destroying al Qaeda in Afghanistan. On that
same night of October 7, however, the United States missed
a crucial opportunity. A surveillance plane spotted the Taliban's leader, Mullah Mohammed Omar, as he fled the
bombing of the capital city of Kabul. The jet could not fire
on Omar without authorization from American Central
Command, or CENTCOM, which guided the battle from
seven thousand miles away in Tampa, Florida. The request
to fire on Omar was not granted, and the U.S. military was
not allowed to fire on the building in which he took refuge.
With no troops on the ground, the United States had no
way of surrounding Omar's refuge and capturing him.

Although the United States used a massive airborne
military arsenal against an enemy with relatively primitive
arms at its disposal, the remoteness of U.S. Central Command led to a missed opportunity in the case of Mullah
Omar. Had troops been on the ground, or had CENT-
COM been closer to the battle, the Taliban's leader might
have been captured or killed at the beginning of combat.
The initial air strikes were intended to weaken the Taliban
forces and to destroy the al Qaeda training camps, but it was
clear to most U.S. military commanders that a ground war
would eventually be necessary to depose the Taliban and destroy al Qaeda. The United States' limited use of its own
ground forces, however, would be a recurrent theme that

would have serious repercussions throughout the Afghan campaign. Fearing heavy casualties and the possibility of appearing to be an invading army, the United States opted for a strategy that relied heavily on using indigenous warlords, most notably the Northern Alliance, to carry out the attack on Afghanistan. The strategy chosen for the U.S.-led attack on Afghanistan did produce a quick victory, but may have also promoted conditions for future strife.

The Fall of the Taliban

The early air strikes on the Taliban between October 7 and October 9, 2001, swiftly gave U.S. aircraft undisputed supremacy in the skies. Between October 9 and October 19, raids were carried out by U.S.-led planes on Taliban strongholds and al Qaeda camps with devastating effect. As the list of viable targets diminished and the prospect of a ground war became imminent, the United States carefully weighed its options. A massive ground assault by U.S.-led troops had been ruled out. No significant anti-Taliban force existed among Afghanistan's dominant ethnic tribe, the Pashtuns, since they were sympathetic to the Taliban's form of Islamic fundamentalism and also because most of the Taliban were Pashtuns themselves. The only viable anti-Taliban Afghan fighting force already on the ground was a loosely united group of ethnic Tajik and Uzbek warlords, known collectively as the Northern Alliance.

These warlords were mostly former mujahideen, or Islamic holy warriors who fought against the Soviets in Afghanistan in the 1980s. They plunged Afghanistan into a devastating civil war following the collapse of a Soviet-backed Afghan Communist regime in the early 1990s. The gruesome, ruthless tactics they employed to fight one another and the way they terrorized and subjugated the Afghan populace contributed to the rise of the Taliban, who offered relative stability compared to the violence of the warlords. With an atrocious human rights record not much better than the Taliban's, the Northern Alliance was the U.S.-led coalition's only choice for indigenous allies in the fight against the Taliban and al Qaeda.

Beginning October 21, 2001, U.S. tactics in Afghanistan markedly changed as U.S. air strikes were launched to support Northern Alliance attacks on the Taliban. As small numbers of U.S. special forces and Central Intelligence Agency agents began to supply money and ammunition to select war-lords, the combined U.S. and Northern Alliance forces advanced on the Taliban front lines. This support, however, was not given wholesale. To prevent the Northern Alliance forces from occupying major cities and seizing political power for themselves, coalition forces provided only necessary material and tactical support. Instead of enormous assaults that would decimate the Taliban and allow the Northern Alliance to capture territory unchecked, small operations were launched against the Taliban with coalition assistance. Northern Alliance fighters identified Taliban and al Qaeda targets on the ground, and the coalition troops used lasers to guide the bombs they dropped from U.S. warplanes to destroy these targets. Over the next month, the United States led bombing campaigns in major cities, including Mazar-e Sharif, Herat, Kandahar, and the capital city of Kabul, to break Taliban and al Qaeda holdouts. At the start of November 2001, with the harsh Afghan winter approaching, the United States decided to intensify the bombing campaign in order to allow indigenous anti-Taliban forces to seize strategic targets.

Once the decision was made to keep bombing during the holy month of Ramadan (a Muslim month of fasting) in order to prevent the Taliban from regrouping or rebuilding demolished fortifications, the Taliban's collapse was rapid. The city of Mazar-e Sharif fell to the Northern Alliance on November 10. The capital city of Kabul fell on November 13, and the Northern Alliance, contrary to the wishes of U.S. commanders, occupied the city. They feared that the Northern Alliance might try to slaughter Pashtun residents of Kabul since most of the Taliban who had ousted the Northern Alliance's mujahideen government in the early 1990s were Pashtuns. The Northern Alliance's occupation of Kabul, however, proved to be relatively peaceful, due in no small part to the U.S. warplanes that flew just overhead. The last Taliban stronghold, the southern city of Kandahar, fell to U.S.-led troops on December 7, 2001. The Taliban and al Qaeda members fled to the cave complexes in the mountains of eastern Afghanistan on the Pakistani border. Their flight effectively ended the rule of the Taliban in Afghanistan.

A delegation of prominent Afghans gathered in Bonn, Germany, early in December 2001, to discuss and ratify an interim government and to sketch out the needs of a war-ravaged Afghanistan. The delegation elected Hamid Karzai,

UZBEKISTAN

TAJIKISTAN

TURKMENISTAN

Amu Darya River

CHINA

IRAN

Pamir Mts.

Kunduz
Nov. 24

Mazar-e Sharif
Nov. 10

Hindu Kush Mts. Wakhan Corridor

Herat
Nov. 12

SALANG PASS

Panjshir Valley

AFGHANISTAN

Kabul
Nov. 13

Bagram

★Shindand
Nov. 12

NORTHWEST
FRONTIER PROVINCE

Jalalabad

KHYBER PASS

Tarin Kowt
Nov. 18

Peshawar

PAKISTAN

Helmand River

Kandahar
Dec. 7

Quetta

**Battles for Afghanistan,
November/December 2001**

an ethnic Pashtun, as the interim president of Afghanistan. However, the use of Northern Alliance troops in the defeat of the Taliban left the U.S. coalition politically beholden to the alliance. As a result, the Pashtun president found his government full of former Tajik and Uzbek warlords. Many of the chief cities and provinces were governed by heavily armed warlords with little or no allegiance to the central government. At the beginning of 2002, however, immediate security and stability, not long-term nation building, were the major considerations. Taliban and al Qaeda forces were still on the run and posed a threat to the new government and the warlords. The coalition and its Afghan allies still had fighting to do.

Operation Anaconda

In March 2002, coalition forces in conjunction with Afghan forces launched Operation Anaconda against several hundred al Qaeda and Taliban members thought to be hiding in the cave complexes in Afghanistan's eastern Paktia Province. Although the operation ultimately proved a success, it also showed the flaws in the coalition's collaboration with indigenous forces. In the first place, local warlords in the Shah-i-Kot Valley area where the raid took place had vied among themselves for power and allowed, whether inadvertently or knowingly, al Qaeda and Taliban members to regroup there. In the lead-up to battle, local villagers claimed that the al Qaeda fighters had received advance notice of the raid from sympathizers in the Afghan force. Afghan forces along with U.S. special forces attempted to flush al Qaeda and Taliban fighters out of their caves and into the valley, but the rebels remained in their positions, even after two days of heavy combat. Seven U.S. soldiers were killed in this early stage of fighting.

Taliban and al Qaeda forces were able to launch hit-and-run attacks against coalition forces for some time, emerging from the caves, attacking, and then returning to the shelter of the cave complexes. It became clear that the coalition forces were fighting against a hardened, determined enemy. It was thought that perhaps top-level al Qaeda or Taliban leaders had taken refuge in the caves, which would explain the ruthless ferocity of the rebel fighters. Though the rebels were heavily armed at the outset of the attack, their ammunition eventually began to run low and coalition forces were able to move within striking distance of the caves. The rebels were reinforced for a while by influxes of fighters who traveled through the mountain passes to the caves, but these reinforcements were cut off when anti-Taliban Afghan forces fanned out around the mountains and blocked the major passes.

The battle ended on March 13 when coalition forces stormed the caves and destroyed them with heavy explosives to prevent their future use. As many as 550 enemy fighters had been killed, but many al Qaeda survivors slipped past the Afghan fighters and fled, most likely into Pakistan. The difficult terrain may explain why some of them were able to get away. Most, however, were able to escape because the Afghans did not have the resources or manpower to stop them. In some cases, Afghans sympathetic to their fellow Muslim fighters let them get away. The U.S. strategy of relying on a mix of indigenous forces and allied soldiers instead of using only professional coalition troops allowed al Qaeda and Taliban members, perhaps even top leaders, to escape.

Following the qualified success of Operation Anaconda, the United States turned its focus to peacekeeping and nation building endeavors in Afghanistan, which are ongoing as of this writing. Military operations are now characterized by limited raids and quelling the minor uprisings of Taliban and al Qaeda insurgents.

Repercussions of Using
Warlords in Coalition Operations

The use of Northern Alliance forces and warlords in the early stages of combat allowed the U.S.-led coalition to topple the Taliban quickly and destroy al Qaeda's central base of operations, from which it launched global terrorist attacks. Moreover, by enlisting the aid of the Northern Alliance, the United States avoided appearing as an invasion force, thereby preventing mass uprisings of the Afghan people, while keeping U.S. casualties at a minimum. These are certainly not small achievements, but they do not convey the whole picture. Collaborating with Northern Alliance forces had and continues to have serious repercussions.

To begin with, using the Northern Alliance to fight al Qaeda and the Taliban meant leaving the warlords heavily armed—indeed, it meant giving them more weapons. Because the United States continues to give monetary and material support to the warlords for their efforts in hunting down the Taliban and al Qaeda, the warlords have little incentive to give up their regional power to the Afghan na-

Accompanied by Afghan boys, a U.S. marine conducts a security patrol in Sarobi, Afghanistan, in May 2004.

tional government. Many of the warlords are not in fact loyal to the Karzai central government. President Karzai is an ethnic Pashtun, whereas most of the warlords are Uzbeks or Tajiks, Afghan ethnic minorities. The regional warlords—entrenched in their territories, loath to disarm, and owing no ethnic allegiance to their leader—weaken and threaten Karzai's regime.

Also, many members of the Northern Alliance practice a fundamentalist form of Islam similar to that of the Taliban. Some local warlords, especially some Pashtun warlords in southern Afghanistan, therefore have sympathy for al Qaeda and the Taliban. This has raised concern among the Afghan population that fundamentalist rule could return to Afghanistan, either in the form of policies handed down by the regional warlords or in the return of Pashtun-supported Taliban rule. The use of warlords helped the U.S.-led coalition depose the Taliban and fragment al Qaeda. However, it may also have created future obstacles to U.S. policy goals in Afghanistan in the form of a destabilized nation, a fearful populace, and the potential for Islamic fundamentalists to rule once again.

The Legacy of the U.S.-Led Attack

The United States has certainly achieved many goals in Afghanistan. The warlords have not, in fact, plunged the country into civil war as they did in the 1990s. Many roads, bridges, irrigation systems, and buildings have been rebuilt. Schools are now open to girls for the first time in many years. A new, stable currency has gone into circulation, replacing several worthless ones. Most importantly, the country enjoys greater freedom than it has in decades, despite warlord interference.

Total and final victory, however, is far from certain. The warlords that the United States has so steadfastly supported in the hunt for al Qaeda often thwart rather than aid the efforts of the coalition and the fledgling Karzai government. Taliban recruitment is on the rise, which would have been impossible if the Taliban had been wiped out or could not find patronage in Afghanistan. The drug trade has sharply increased as warlords seek to increase gains for themselves and to fund military activities against al Qaeda and against one another. Also, foreign regional powers, including Iran, Russia, and Pakistan, seek to advance their interests in Afghanistan by backing various rival warlord factions. As the warlords try to consolidate their power and dominate their provinces, human rights violations are still rampant, with women and girls suffering the most.

The United States attacked Afghanistan in order to remove the fundamentalist Taliban government and to destroy al Qaeda in Afghanistan. While these goals were achieved in the short term, U.S. sponsorship of the warlords has fostered instability similar to that which first allowed for the rise of Islamic fundamentalist rule and terrorist activity in Afghanistan. History will show whether the U.S. attack on Afghanistan had a lasting positive effect on that war-ravaged nation and the world at large. The following chapters explore the U.S. attack on Afghanistan and its legacy.

Chapter 1

Debating the Case for War

1

America Must Attack Afghanistan to Fight Terrorism

George W. Bush

In a speech to the United Nations General Assembly on November 10, 2001, President George W. Bush states that Afghanistan is under attack because its Taliban regime harbored and supported the terrorists responsible for the attacks of September 11, 2001. He appeals to all nations to join the United States in its fight against terrorism. He also emphasizes that the attack on Afghanistan is just the first battle in a global war against terror.

M r. Secretary General, Mr. President [of UN General Assembly], distinguished delegates, and ladies and gentlemen. We meet in a hall devoted to peace, in a city scarred by violence, in a nation awakened to danger, in a world uniting for a long struggle. Every civilized nation here today is resolved to keep the most basic commitment of civilization: We will defend ourselves and our future against terror and lawless violence.

The United Nations was founded in this cause. In a second world war, we learned there is no isolation from evil. We affirmed that some crimes are so terrible they offend humanity, itself. And we resolved that the aggressions and ambitions of the wicked must be opposed early, decisively, and collectively, before they threaten us all. That evil has re-

George W. Bush, address to the UN General Assembly, New York, November 10, 2001.

turned, and that cause is renewed.

A few miles from here, many thousands still lie in a tomb of rubble. Tomorrow, the Secretary General, the President of the General Assembly, and I will visit that site [of the World Trade Center], where the names of every nation and region that lost citizens will be read aloud. If we were to read the names of every person who died, it would take more than three hours.

Those names include a citizen of Gambia, whose wife spent their fourth wedding anniversary, September the 12th, searching in vain for her husband. Those names include a man who supported his wife in Mexico, sending home money every week. Those names include a young Pakistani who prayed toward Mecca five times a day, and died that day trying to save others.

Terrorism Affects the Entire World

The suffering of September the 11th [2001] was inflicted on people of many faiths and many nations. All of the victims, including Muslims, were killed with equal indifference and equal satisfaction by the terrorist leaders. The terrorists are violating the tenets of every religion, including the one they invoke.

Last week, the Sheikh of Al-Azhar University, the world's oldest Islamic institution of higher learning, declared that terrorism is a disease, and that Islam prohibits killing innocent civilians. The terrorists call their cause holy, yet, they fund it with drug dealing; they encourage murder and suicide in the name of a great faith that forbids both. They dare to ask God's blessing as they set out to kill innocent men, women and children. But the God of Isaac and Ishmael would never answer such a prayer. And a murderer is not a martyr; he is just a murderer.

We act to defend ourselves and deliver our children from a future of fear.

Time is passing. Yet, for the United States of America, there will be no forgetting September the 11th. We will remember every rescuer who died in honor. We will remember every family that lives in grief. We will remember the fire and ash, the last phone calls, the funerals of the children.

And the people of my country will remember those who have plotted against us. We are learning their names. We are coming to know their faces. There is no corner of the Earth distant or dark enough to protect them. However long it takes, their hour of justice will come.

In this war of terror, each of us must answer for what we have done or what we have left undone.

Every nation has a stake in this cause. As we meet, the terrorists are planning more murder—perhaps in my country, or perhaps in yours. They kill because they aspire to dominate. They seek to overthrow governments and destabilize entire regions.

Last week, anticipating this meeting of the General Assembly, they denounced the United Nations. They called our Secretary General a criminal and condemned all Arab nations here as traitors to Islam.

Few countries meet their exacting standards of brutality and oppression. Every other country is a potential target. And all the world faces the most horrifying prospect of all: These same terrorists are searching for weapons of mass destruction, the tools to turn their hatred into holocaust. They can be expected to use chemical, biological and nuclear weapons the moment they are capable of doing so. No hint of conscience would prevent it.

This threat cannot be ignored. This threat cannot be appeased. Civilization itself, the civilization we share, is threatened. History will record our response, and judge or justify every nation in this hall.

Defending the World from Terror

The civilized world is now responding. We act to defend ourselves and deliver our children from a future of fear. We choose the dignity of life over a culture of death. We choose lawful change and civil disagreement over coercion, subversion, and chaos. These commitments—hope and order, law and life—unite people across cultures and continents. Upon these commitments depend all peace and progress. For these commitments, we are determined to fight.

The United Nations has risen to this responsibility. On the 12th of September, these buildings opened for emergency meetings of the General Assembly and the Security Council. Before the sun had set, these attacks on the world stood condemned by the world. And I want to thank you for this strong and principled stand.

I also thank the Arab Islamic countries that have condemned terrorist murder. Many of you have seen the destruction of terror in your own lands. The terrorists are increasingly isolated by their own hatred and extremism. They cannot hide behind Islam. The authors of mass murder and their allies have no place in any culture, and no home in any faith.

The conspiracies of terror are being answered by an expanding global coalition. Not every nation will be a part of every action against the enemy. But every nation in our coalition has duties. These duties can be demanding, as we in America are learning. We have already made adjustments in our laws and in our daily lives. We're taking new measures to investigate terror and to protect against threats.

The leaders of all nations must now carefully consider their responsibilities and their future. Terrorist groups like al Qaeda depend upon the aid or indifference of governments. They need the support of a financial infrastructure, and safe havens to train and plan and hide.

Some nations want to play their part in the fight against terror, but tell us they lack the means to enforce their laws and control their borders. We stand ready to help. Some governments still turn a blind eye to the terrorists, hoping the threat will pass them by. They are mistaken. And some governments, while pledging to uphold the principles of the U.N., have cast their lot with the terrorists. They support them and harbor them, and they will find that their welcome guests are parasites that will weaken them, and eventually consume them.

For every regime that sponsors terror, there is a price to be paid. And it will be paid. The allies of terror are equally guilty of murder and equally accountable to justice.

U.S. Military Action in Afghanistan

The Taliban are now learning this lesson—that regime and the terrorists who support it are now virtually indistinguishable. Together they promote terror abroad and impose a reign of terror on the Afghan people. Women are executed in Kabul's soccer stadium. They can be beaten for wearing socks that are too thin. Men are jailed for missing prayer meetings.

The United States, supported by many nations, is bringing justice to the terrorists in Afghanistan. We're making progress against military targets, and that is our objective. Unlike the enemy, we seek to minimize, not maximize, the loss of innocent life.

There is no such thing as a good terrorist. No national aspiration, no remembered wrong can ever justify the deliberate murder of the innocent.

I'm proud of the honorable conduct of the American military. And my country grieves for all the suffering the Taliban have brought upon Afghanistan, including the terrible burden of war. The Afghan people do not deserve their present rulers. Years of Taliban misrule have brought nothing but misery and starvation. Even before this current crisis, 4 million Afghans depended on food from the United States and other nations, and millions of Afghans were refugees from Taliban oppression.

I make this promise to all the victims of that regime: The Taliban's days of harboring terrorists and dealing in heroin and brutalizing women are drawing to a close. And when that regime is gone, the people of Afghanistan will say with the rest of the world: good riddance.

I can promise, too, that America will join the world in helping the people of Afghanistan rebuild their country. Many nations, including mine, are sending food and medicine to help Afghans through the winter. America has air-dropped over 1.3 million packages of rations into Afghanistan. Just this week, we air-lifted 20,000 blankets and over 200 tons of provisions into the region. We continue to provide humanitarian aid, even while the Taliban tries to steal the food we send.

More help eventually will be needed. The United States will work closely with the United Nations and development banks to reconstruct Afghanistan after hostilities there have ceased and the Taliban are no longer in control. And the United States will work with the U.N. to support a post-Taliban government that represents all of the Afghan people.

Global Efforts Against Terror

In this war of terror, each of us must answer for what we have done or what we have left undone. After tragedy, there is a time for sympathy and condolence. And my country has been very grateful for both. The memorials and vigils around the world will not be forgotten. But the time for sympathy has now passed; the time for action has now arrived.

The most basic obligations in this new conflict have already been defined by the United Nations. On September the 28th, the Security Council adopted Resolution 1373. Its requirements are clear: Every United Nations member has a responsibility to crack down on terrorist financing. We must pass all necessary laws in our own countries to allow the confiscation of terrorist assets. We must apply those laws to every financial institution in every nation.

We have a responsibility to share intelligence and coordinate the efforts of law enforcement. If you know something, tell us. If we know something, we'll tell you. And when we find the terrorists, we must work together to bring them to justice. We have a responsibility to deny any sanctuary, safe haven or transit to terrorists. Every known terrorist camp must be shut down, its operators apprehended, and evidence of their arrest presented to the United Nations. We have a responsibility to deny weapons to terrorists and to actively prevent private citizens from providing them.

It is our task—the task of this generation—to provide the response to aggression and terror.

These obligations are urgent and they are binding on every nation with a place in this chamber. Many governments are taking these obligations seriously, and my country appreciates it. Yet, even beyond Resolution 1373, more is required, and more is expected of our coalition against terror.

We're asking for a comprehensive commitment to this fight. We must unite in opposing all terrorists, not just some of them. In this world there are good causes and bad causes, and we may disagree on where the line is drawn. Yet, there is no such thing as a good terrorist. No national aspiration, no remembered wrong can ever justify the deliberate murder of the innocent. Any government that rejects this principle, trying to pick and choose its terrorist friends, will know the consequences.

No Agenda but Fighting Terrorism

We must speak the truth about terror. Let us never tolerate outrageous conspiracy theories concerning the attacks of September the 11th; malicious lies that attempt to shift the blame away from the terrorists, themselves, away from the guilty. To inflame ethnic hatred is to advance the cause of terror.

The war against terror must not serve as an excuse to persecute ethnic and religious minorities in any country. Innocent people must be allowed to live their own lives, by their own customs, under their own religion. And every nation must have avenues for the peaceful expression of opinion and dissent. When these avenues are closed, the temptation to speak through violence grows.

We must press on with our agenda for peace and prosperity in every land. My country is pledged to encouraging development and expanding trade. My country is pledged to investing in education and combatting AIDS and other infectious diseases around the world. Following September 11th, these pledges are even more important. In our struggle against hateful groups that exploit poverty and despair, we must offer an alternative of opportunity and hope.

The American government also stands by its commitment to a just peace in the Middle East. We are working toward a day when two states, Israel and Palestine, live peacefully together within secure and recognized borders as called for by the Security Council resolutions. We will do all in our power to bring both parties back into negotiations. But peace will only come when all have sworn off, forever, incitement, violence and terror.

And, finally, this struggle is a defining moment for the United Nations, itself. And the world needs its principled leadership. It undermines the credibility of this great institution, for example, when the Commission on Human Rights offers seats to the world's most persistent violators of human rights. The United Nations depends, above all, on its moral authority—and that authority must be preserved.

A Hard Fight Ahead

The steps I described will not be easy. For all nations, they will require effort. For some nations, they will require great courage. Yet, the cost of inaction is far greater. The only alternative to victory is a nightmare world where every city is a potential killing field.

As I've told the American people, freedom and fear are at war. We face enemies that hate not our policies, but our existence; the tolerance of openness and creative culture that defines us. But the outcome of this conflict is certain: There is a current in history and it runs toward freedom. Our enemies resent it and dismiss it, but the dreams of mankind are defined by liberty—the natural right to create and build and worship and live in dignity. When men and women are released from oppression and isolation, they find fulfillment and hope, and they leave poverty by the millions.

These aspirations are lifting up the peoples of Europe, Asia, Africa and the Americas, and they can lift up all of the Islamic world.

We stand for the permanent hopes of humanity, and those hopes will not be denied. We're confident, too, that history has an author who fills time and eternity with his purpose. We know that evil is real, but good will prevail against it. This is the teaching of many faiths, and in that assurance we gain strength for a long journey.

It is our task—the task of this generation—to provide the response to aggression and terror. We have no other choice, because there is no other peace.

We did not ask for this mission, yet there is honor in history's call. We have a chance to write the story of our times, a story of courage defeating cruelty and light overcoming darkness. This calling is worthy of any life, and worthy of every nation. So let us go forward, confident, determined, and unafraid.

2

A U.S. Attack on Afghanistan Is Simply Vengeance

Arundhati Roy

In the days following the September 11, 2001, attacks in New York and Washington, it was unclear why the attacks occurred or who carried them out. In the following article, Indian novelist Arundhati Roy points out the pitfalls of rushing headlong into war before all the facts are known. She argues that although the grief of the American people is a natural reaction to the tragedy, a military attack against the Afghan people is completely unjustified. Roy states that American policies may have contributed to the September 11 attacks and asserts that the people of Afghanistan are not the rightful recipients of American wrath. Roy is the author of *The God of Small Things*, which won a Booker Prize in 1997.

I n the aftermath of the unconscionable September 11 suicide attacks on the Pentagon and the World Trade Centre, an American newscaster said: "Good and evil rarely manifest themselves as clearly as they did last Tuesday. People who we don't know massacred people who we do. And they did so with contemptuous glee." Then he broke down and wept.

Here's the rub: America is at war against people it doesn't know, because they don't appear much on TV. Before it has properly identified or even begun to comprehend the nature of its enemy, the US government has, in a rush of publicity and embarrassing rhetoric, cobbled together an "international coalition against terror", mobilised its army, its air force, its navy and its media, and committed them to battle.

The trouble is that once America goes off to war, it can't very well return without having fought one. If it doesn't find its enemy, for the sake of the enraged folks back home, it will have to manufacture one. Once war begins, it will develop a momentum, a logic and a justification of its own, and we'll lose sight of why it's being fought in the first place.

What we're witnessing here is the spectacle of the world's most powerful country reaching reflexively, angrily, for an old instinct to fight a new kind of war. Suddenly, when it comes to defending itself, America's streamlined warships, cruise missiles and F-16 jets look like obsolete, lumbering things. As deterrence, its arsenal of nuclear bombs is no longer worth its weight in scrap. Box-cutters, penknives, and cold anger are the weapons with which the wars of the new century will be waged. Anger is the lock pick. It slips through customs unnoticed. Doesn't show up in baggage checks.

Misconstruing the Threat

Who is America fighting? On September 20, the FBI said that it had doubts about the identities of some of the hijackers. On the same day President George Bush said, "We know exactly who these people are and which governments are supporting them." It sounds as though the president knows something that the FBI and the American public don't.

In his September 20 address to the US Congress, President Bush called the enemies of America "enemies of freedom". "Americans are asking, 'Why do they hate us?'" he said. "They hate our freedoms—our freedom of religion, our freedom of speech, our freedom to vote and assemble and disagree with each other." People are being asked to make two leaps of faith here. First, to assume that The Enemy is who the US government says it is, even though it has no substantial evidence to support that claim. And second, to assume that The Enemy's motives are what the US government says they are, and there's nothing to support that either.

For strategic, military and economic reasons, it is vital for the US government to persuade its public that their commitment to freedom and democracy and the American Way of Life is under attack. In the current atmosphere of grief, outrage and anger, it's an easy notion to peddle. However, if that were true, it's reasonable to wonder why the symbols of America's economic and military dominance—the World Trade Centre and the Pentagon—were chosen as the targets of the attacks. Why not the Statue of Liberty? Could it be that the stygian anger that led to the attacks has its taproot not in American freedom and democracy, but in the US government's record of commitment and support to exactly the opposite things—to military and economic terrorism, insurgency, military dictatorship, religious bigotry and unimaginable genocide (outside America)? It must be hard for ordinary Americans, so recently bereaved, to look up at the world with their eyes full of tears and encounter what might appear to them to be indifference. It isn't indifference. It's just augury. An absence of surprise. The tired wisdom of knowing that what goes around eventually comes around. American people ought to know that it is not them but their government's policies that are so hated. They can't possibly doubt that they themselves, their extraordinary musicians, their writers, their actors, their spectacular sportsmen and their cinema, are universally welcomed. All of us have been moved by the courage and grace shown by firefighters, rescue workers and ordinary office staff in the days since the attacks.

America's grief at what happened has been immense and immensely public. It would be grotesque to expect it to calibrate or modulate its anguish. However, it will be a pity if, instead of using this as an opportunity to try to understand why September 11 happened, Americans use it as an opportunity to usurp the whole world's sorrow to mourn and avenge only their own. Because then it falls to the rest of us to ask the hard questions and say the harsh things. And for our pains, for our bad timing, we will be disliked, ignored and perhaps eventually silenced.

The Impulse to Take Action

The world will probably never know what motivated those particular hijackers who flew planes into those particular American buildings. They were not glory boys. They left no suicide notes, no political messages; no organisation has claimed credit for the attacks. All we know is that their belief in what they were doing outstripped the natural human instinct for survival, or any desire to be remembered. It's al-

most as though they could not scale down the enormity of
their rage to anything smaller than their deeds. And what
they did has blown a hole in the world as we knew it. In the
absence of information, politicians, political commentators
and writers (like myself) will invest the act with their own
politics, with their own interpretations. This speculation,
this analysis of the political climate in which the attacks took
place, can only be a good thing.

---

*It's reasonable to wonder why the symbols of
America's economic and military dominance . . .
were chosen as the targets of the attacks.*

But war is looming large. Whatever remains to be said
must be said quickly. Before America places itself at the
helm of the "international coalition against terror", before
it invites (and coerces) countries to actively participate in its
almost godlike mission—called Operation Infinite Justice
until it was pointed out that this could be seen as an insult
to Muslims, who believe that only Allah can mete out infinite justice, and was renamed Operation Enduring Freedom—it would help if some small clarifications are made.
For example, infinite Justice/Enduring Freedom for whom?
Is this America's war against terror in America or against
terror in general? What exactly is being avenged here? Is it
the tragic loss of almost 7,000 lives, the gutting of five million square feet of office space in Manhattan, the destruction of a section of the Pentagon, the loss of several hundreds of thousands of jobs, the bankruptcy of some airline
companies and the dip in the New York Stock Exchange?
Or is it more than that? In 1996, Madeleine Albright, then
the US secretary of state, was asked on national television
what she felt about the fact that 500,000 Iraqi children had
died as a result of US economic sanctions. She replied that
it was "a very hard choice", but that, all things considered,
"we think the price is worth it". Albright never lost her job
for saying this. She continued to travel the world representing the views and aspirations of the US government. . . .
  So here we have it. The equivocating distinction between civilisation and savagery, between the "massacre of
innocent people" or, if you like, "a clash of civilisations" and

"collateral damage". The sophistry and fastidious algebra of infinite justice. How many dead Iraqis will it take to make the world a better place? How many dead Afghans for every dead American? How many dead women and children for every dead man? How many dead mojahedin for each dead investment banker? As we watch mesmerised, Operation Enduring Freedom unfolds on TV monitors across the world. A coalition of the world's superpowers is closing in on Afghanistan, one of the poorest, most ravaged, war-torn, countries in the world, whose ruling [Islamic fundamentalist] Taliban government is sheltering Osama bin Laden, the men being held responsible for the September 11 attacks.

Targeting Afghanistan

The only thing in Afghanistan that could possibly count as collateral value is its citizenry. (Among them, half a million maimed orphans. There are accounts of hobbling stampedes that occur when artificial limbs are airdropped into remote, inaccessible villages.) Afghanistan's economy is in a shambles. In fact, the problem for an invading army is that Afghanistan has no conventional coordinates or signposts to plot on a military map—no big cities, no highways, no industrial complexes, no water treatment plants. Farms have been turned into mass graves. The countryside is littered with land mines—10 million is the most recent estimate. The American army would first have to clear the mines and build roads in order to take its soldiers in.

A coalition of the world's superpowers is closing in on Afghanistan, one of the poorest, most ravaged, war-torn countries in the world.

Fearing an attack from America, one million citizens have fled from their homes and arrived at the border between Pakistan and Afghanistan. The UN estimates that there are eight million Afghan citizens who need emergency aid. As supplies run out—food and aid agencies have been asked to leave—the BBC reports that one of the worst humanitarian disasters of recent times has begun to unfold. Witness the infinite justice of the new century. Civilians starving to death while they're waiting to be killed.

In America there has been rough talk of "bombing Afghanistan back to the stone age". Someone please break the news that Afghanistan is already there. And if it's any consolation, America played no small part in helping it on its way. The American people may be a little fuzzy about where exactly Afghanistan is (we hear reports that there's a run on maps of the country), but the US government and Afghanistan are old friends.

History of US Intervention in Afghanistan

In 1979, after the Soviet invasion of Afghanistan, the CIA and Pakistan's ISI (Inter Services Intelligence [Pakistan's intelligence agency]) launched the largest covert operation in the history of the CIA. Their purpose was to harness the energy of Afghan resistance to the Soviets and expand it into a holy war, an Islamic jihad, which would turn Muslim countries within the Soviet Union against the communist regime and eventually destabilise it. When it began, it was meant to be the Soviet Union's Vietnam. It turned out to be much more than that. Over the years, through the ISI, the CIA funded and recruited almost 100,000 radical mojahedin from 40 Islamic countries as soldiers for America's proxy war. The rank and file of the mojahedin were unaware that their jihad [holy war] was actually being fought on behalf of Uncle Sam. (The irony is that America was equally unaware that it was financing a future war against itself.)

In 1989, after being bloodied by 10 years of relentless conflict, the Russians withdrew, leaving behind a civilisation reduced to rubble.

Civil war in Afghanistan raged on. The jihad spread to Chechnya, Kosovo and eventually to Kashmir. The CIA continued to pour in money and military equipment, but the overheads had become immense, and more money was needed. The mojahedin ordered farmers to plant opium as a "revolutionary tax". The ISI set up hundreds of heroin laboratories across Afghanistan. Within two years of the CIA's arrival, the Pakistan-Afghanistan borderland had become the biggest producer of heroin in the world, and the single biggest source of the heroin on American streets. The annual profits, said to be between $100bn and $200bn, were ploughed back into training and arming militants.

In 1995, the Taliban—then a marginal sect of dangerous, hardline fundamentalists—fought its way to power in

Afghanistan. It was funded by the ISI, that old cohort of the CIA, and supported by many political parties in Pakistan. The Taliban unleashed a regime of terror. Its first victims were its own people, particularly women. It closed down girls' schools, dismissed women from government jobs, and enforced sharia laws[1] under which women deemed to be "immoral" are stoned to death, and widows guilty of being adulterous are buried alive. Given the Taliban government's human rights track record, it seems unlikely that it will in any way be intimidated or swerved from its purpose by the prospect of war, or the threat to the lives of its civilians.

Sectarian violence, globalisation's structural adjustment programmes and drug lords are tearing the country to pieces.

After all that has happened, can there be anything more ironic than Russia and America joining hands to re-destroy Afghanistan? The question is, can you destroy destruction? Dropping more bombs on Afghanistan will only shuffle the rubble, scramble some old graves and disturb the dead.

The desolate landscape of Afghanistan was the burial ground of Soviet communism and the springboard of a unipolar world dominated by America. It made the space for neocapitalism and corporate globalisation, again dominated by America. And now Afghanistan is poised to become the graveyard for the unlikely soldiers who fought and won this war for America.

Other Countries Have Been Affected by US Afghan Policies

And what of America's trusted ally? Pakistan too has suffered enormously. The US government has not been shy of supporting military dictators who have blocked the idea of democracy from taking root in the country. Before the CIA arrived, there was a small rural market for opium in Pakistan. Between 1979 and 1985, the number of heroin addicts grew from zero to one-and-a-half million. Even before September 11, there were three million Afghan refugees living in tented camps along the border. Pakistan's economy is

---

1. laws based on the Koran and the sayings and acts of the prophet Muhammad

crumbling. Sectarian violence, globalisation's structural adjustment programmes and drug lords are tearing the country to pieces. Set up to fight the Soviets, the terrorist training centres and madrasahs, sown like dragon's teeth across the country, produced fundamentalists with tremendous popular appeal within Pakistan itself. The Taliban, which the Pakistan government has supported, funded and propped up for years, has material and strategic alliances with Pakistan's own political parties.

Operation Enduring Freedom is ostensibly being fought to uphold the American Way of Life. It'll probably end up undermining it completely.

Now the US government is asking (asking?) Pakistan to garotte the pet it has hand-reared in its backyard for so many years. Pakistani President Musharraf, having pledged his support to the US, could well find he has something resembling civil war on his hands.

India, thanks in part to its geography, and in part to the vision of its former leaders, has so far been fortunate enough to be left out of this Great Game. Had it been drawn in, it's more than likely that our democracy, such as it is, would not have survived. Today, as some of us watch in horror, the Indian government is furiously gyrating its hips, begging the US to set up its base in India rather than Pakistan. Having had this ringside view of Pakistan's sordid fate, it isn't just odd, it's unthinkable, that India should want to do this. Any third world country with a fragile economy and a complex social base should know by now that to invite a superpower such as America in (whether it says it's staying or just passing through) would be like inviting a brick to drop through your windscreen.

A World in Turmoil

Operation Enduring Freedom is ostensibly being fought to uphold the American Way of Life. It'll probably end up undermining it completely. It will spawn more anger and more terror across the world. For ordinary people in America, it will mean lives lived in a climate of sickening uncertainty: will my child be safe in school? Will there be nerve gas in the subway? A bomb in the cinema hall? Will my love come home tonight? There have been warnings about the possibility of biological warfare—smallpox, bubonic plague, anthrax—the deadly payload of innocuous crop-duster aircraft. Being picked off a few at a time may end up being worse than being annihilated all at once by a nuclear bomb.

The US government, and no doubt governments all over the world, will use the climate of war as an excuse to curtail civil liberties, deny free speech, lay off workers, harass ethnic and religious minorities, cut back on public spending and divert huge amounts of money to the defence industry. To what purpose? President Bush can no more "rid the world of evil-doers" than he can stock it with saints. It's absurd for the US government to even toy with the notion that it can stamp out terrorism with more violence and oppression. Terrorism is the symptom, not the disease. Terrorism has no country. It's transnational, as global an enterprise as Coke or Pepsi or Nike. At the first sign of trouble, terrorists can pull up stakes and move their "factories" from country to country in search of a better deal. Just like the multi-nationals.

From all accounts, it will be impossible to produce evidence . . . to link Bin Laden to the September 11 attacks.

Terrorism as a phenomenon may never go away. But if it is to be contained, the first step is for America to at least acknowledge that it shares the planet with other nations, with other human beings who, even if they are not on TV, have loves and griefs and stories and songs and sorrows and, for heaven's sake, rights. Instead, when Donald Rumsfeld, the US defence secretary, was asked what he would call a victory in America's new war, he said that if he could convince the world that Americans must be allowed to continue with their way of life, he would consider it a victory.

The September 11 attacks were a monstrous calling card from a world gone horribly wrong. The message may have been written by Bin Laden (who knows?) and delivered by his couriers, but it could well have been signed by the ghosts of the victims of America's old wars. The millions

killed in Korea, Vietnam and Cambodia, the 17,500 killed
when Israel—backed by the US—invaded Lebanon in 1982,
the 200,000 Iraqis killed in Operation Desert Storm, the
thousands of Palestinians who have died fighting Israel's occupation of the West Bank. And the millions who died, in
Yugoslavia, Somalia, Haiti, Chile, Nicaragua, El Salvador,
the Dominican Republic, Panama, at the hands of all the
terrorists, dictators and genocidists whom the American
government supported, trained, bankrolled and supplied
with arms. And this is far from being a comprehensive list.

For a country involved in so much warfare and conflict,
the American people have been extremely fortunate. The
strikes on September 11 were only the second on American
soil in over a century. The first was Pearl Harbour. The
reprisal for this took a long route, but ended with Hi-
roshima and Nagasaki. This time the world waits with bated
breath for the horrors to come.

America's Relationship with Bin Laden

Someone recently said that if Osama bin Laden didn't exist,
America would have had to invent him. But, in a way, America did invent him. He was among the jihadis who moved to
Afghanistan in 1979 when the CIA commenced its operations there. Bin Laden has the distinction of being created
by the CIA and wanted by the FBI. In the course of a fort-
night he has been promoted from suspect to prime suspect
and then, despite the lack of any real evidence, straight up
the charts to being "wanted dead or alive".

From all accounts, it will be impossible to produce evidence (of the sort that would stand scrutiny in a court of
law) to link Bin Laden to the September 11 attacks. So far,
it appears that the most incriminating piece of evidence
against him is the fact that he has not condemned them.

From what is known about the location of Bin Laden
and the living conditions in which he operates, it's entirely
possible that he did not personally plan and carry out the attacks—that he is the inspirational figure, "the CEO of the
holding company". The Taliban's response to US demands
for the extradition of Bin Laden has been uncharacteristi-
cally reasonable: produce the evidence, then we'll hand him
over. President Bush's response is that the demand is "non-
negotiable".

But who is Osama bin Laden really? Let me rephrase

that. What is Osama bin Laden? He's America's family secret. He is the American president's dark doppelganger. The savage twin of all that purports to be beautiful and civilised. He has been sculpted from the spare rib of a world laid to waste by America's foreign policy: its gunboat diplomacy, its nuclear arsenal, its vulgarly stated policy of "full-spectrum dominance", its chilling disregard for non-American lives, its barbarous military interventions, its support for despotic and dictatorial regimes, its merciless economic agenda that has munched through the economies of poor countries like a cloud of locusts. Its marauding multinationals who are taking over the air we breathe, the ground we stand on, the water we drink, the thoughts we think. Now that the family secret has been spilled, the twins are blurring into one another and gradually becoming interchangeable. Their guns, bombs, money and drugs have been going around in the loop for a while. (The Stinger missiles that will greet US helicopters were supplied by the CIA. The heroin used by America's drug addicts comes from Afghanistan. The Bush administration recently gave Afghanistan a $43m subsidy for a "war on drugs". . . .)

Now Bush and Bin Laden have even begun to borrow each other's rhetoric. Each refers to the other as "the head of the snake". Both invoke God and use the loose millenarian currency of good and evil as their terms of reference. Both are engaged in unequivocal political crimes. Both are dangerously armed—one with the nuclear arsenal of the obscenely powerful, the other with the incandescent, destructive power of the utterly hopeless. The fireball and the ice pick. The bludgeon and the axe. The important thing to keep in mind is that neither is an acceptable alternative to the other.

President Bush's ultimatum to the people of the world— "If you're not with us, you're against us"—is a piece of presumptuous arrogance. It's not a choice that people want to, need to, or should have to make.

3

The United States Must Use Peaceful Means to Root Out Terrorists in Afghanistan

Vladimir Mukhin and Mark Najarian, with Riju D. Mehta

Afghanistan has been strategically important to foreign powers for centuries as a land bridge between Europe and Asia. It also has been notoriously difficult if not impossible to subdue. In the nineteenth century, Britain and Russia became embroiled in a struggle for the region that became known as the Great Game. In the twentieth century, Russia again was pulled into conflict in Afghanistan, only to withdraw several years later after suffering heavy military and financial losses. In this selection, Vladimir Mukhin, Mark Najarian, and Riju D. Mehta analyze the U.S. involvement in Afghanistan and attempt to draw some lessons from history. They explain that the United States is entering the same quagmire that ensnared Russia. Relying too heavily on indigenous troops and alienating the Muslim world by dropping bombs on innocent civilians could ultimately cost the United States the war on terror. The authors argue that the United States must try to understand the customs and ethnic peculiarities of the region or else face an unexpected and harsh defeat. Mukhin is a correspondent for Russia's *Nezavisimaya Gazeta* (Independent Gazette). Najarian is the editor of *Russian Journal.*

Vladimir Mukhin and Mark Najarian, with Riju D. Mehta, "Russian Experience: History's Pointers," *India Today*, November 5, 2001. Copyright © 2001 by Living Media India Ltd., *India Today*. Reproduced by permission.

Nemesis is an ugly word, vicious and wilful, decimating with impunity many an overweening autocrat and ambitious superpower. In an air thick with American vindication, so goes the unspoken thought: America's nemesis could well be lurking in the treacherous terrain of Afghanistan, among the war-hardy [Islamic fundamentalist] Taliban troops and the disparate ethnic structure of its society. The alarm stems from a country that learnt its lesson well in a 10-year campaign in Afghanistan: a conflict that led to 14,453 deaths, a humiliating withdrawal and, some say, the eventual breakup of the Soviet Union. So, is America treading the beaten track only to entrench itself deeper in the Afghan quagmire? Is it pursuing a prudent strategy to root out terrorism? And does it have a viable alternative to the Taliban? The answers may be elusive but those coming from the Russians are laced with credibility.

"The bombing must stop,". . . as it is setting the Muslim world against the US.

"The US seems to be repeating our mistakes," says General Makhmud Gareyev. "Before going in there, they should have decided who they must align with." He should know. Gareyev spent two years as chief military adviser to Afghan president Najibullah and was the head of the armed forces after Soviet troops withdrew in 1989. He has also authored books and articles on the Soviet experience in Afghanistan and is currently the president of the Russian Military Academy of Sciences.

"The Americans give the impression they are pinning their hopes on the Northern Alliance," says Gareyev, "but these troops could, at best, liberate provinces populated by Tajiks and Uzbeks. These minorities won't be able to control the whole of Afghanistan." The Pashtoons who make up over half the population won't accept this. And even if the US succeeds in removing the current Taliban regime, replacing it with "good Taliban," they will still face problems after the military campaign ends. Which is obvious in the rise of the anti-American sentiment in Pakistan and Afghanistan, says Gareyev. "After the bombings, religious people will become more passionate."

In which case, former Afghan king Zahir Shah would be

a neutral figure who could get broad support, says Gareyev. But the US failed to inform him about the anti-terrorist operations even though the king is known to have opposed the bombings in Afghanistan.

Using Peaceful Means to Achieve Goals

"The bombing must stop," agrees Colonel Roman Sudjayev, as it is setting the Muslim world against the US. The Taliban is ready to sit at the negotiating table and talk about a coalition government, affirms the man who served in Afghanistan in 1987-88 as deputy head of a medical battalion. Once this happens, they will need economic aid and investment, so the US and other developed countries should prove to Afghanistan and other Muslim nations that they are friends by providing economic help.

"Only through peaceful means, through consensus, dialogue and good deeds will the US be able to root out Muslim terrorism in Afghanistan and the world," says Sudjayev who has also worked in command posts in the Defence and Emergency Situations ministries and is a leading researcher at the Institute for the Development of Social Partnership.

"The whole world is fighting terrorism, not just the US."

If rooting out the terrorist groups is the aim, says Gareyev, then there are ways of achieving this, but if the aim is to change the situation in the country and get rid of the Taliban, then this requires large-scale action. A military offensive may not be the best option considering the Taliban's history and the means they used to gain power in the first place. They assumed control of 90 per cent of the territory not through gun battles but by buying tribal and ethnic loyalties. According to Gareyev, if the Americans "realise how important it is to buy people and begin to give money to the anti-Taliban coalition, they'll be able to do in the terrorists more quickly".

"Afghanistan has its own customs and traditions," recounts the general citing an instance. Najibullah had so-called tribal regiments in his armed forces comprising members of a particular group or tribe. On a business trip to Shindant where one of the regiments was based, he discovered that the regiment had suddenly shifted allegiance to the mujahideen [who fought against the Soviets in the 1980s]. "We had to bargain and persuade them to let us go by promising them arms," he says, underlining the need for the US to adopt alternative strategies.

General Mikhail Moiseyev agrees military action alone cannot defeat terrorism. "The whole world is fighting terrorism, not just the US," says the former head of the Russian military's General Headquarters (1991) and current Defence Ministry adviser and member of the government Commission on Social Problems of Servicemen. "We also need to take diplomatic and economic steps against terrorist organisations. Intelligence services also have a major role to play here."

Application of Military Tactics

Especially in ground operations. "If troop positions are disguised or if they are hiding in caves, satellite intelligence won't find them," asserts Gareyev. Air strikes alone will not help the US catch all the terrorists even if they fight for many years because of the country's difficult terrain—mountains, deserts and caves. So effective intelligence is a must if the US is to make progress on the ground. The US special forces tried to carry out a number of ground operations, but I think they were unsuccessful, speculates Gareyev. So while the US may be able to destroy stockpiles, groups of troops, command points, anti-aircraft defenses and artillery positions, it is impossible to track an individual down as he moves across towns through irrigation canals. Nearly every town has hundreds of kilometres of such canals three to four metres deep and are covered with earth, reveals Gareyev.

The ground operations may also be affected by the onset of winter though this is unlikely to affect the air strikes. "Winter isn't a problem for modern aircraft or missiles," says Gareyev. "The air strikes will continue and there will be support for the anti-Taliban forces. As for continued operations during Ramadan[1] (in November), the Pentagon hasn't taken a decision yet," he adds. Moiseyev believes the Taliban and its opponents are unlikely to fight on the ground

1. U.S. forces stopped bombing during Ramadan but continued with military operations.

during the Muslim holy month. And though Pakistani President General Pervez Musharraf has spoken in favour of halting the bombing during Ramadan, US Secretary of State Colin Powell has put off the decision saying America would take into account not just military but also diplomatic considerations.

Sudjayev, meanwhile, is worried about the length of the military operations. "I think the anti-terrorist operations have already become drawn out. Active fighting can probably get under way only in late winter or early spring once the Islamic holidays are over and the snow melts," he speculates.

As for the success that America is likely to achieve in waging its war against terrorism in Afghanistan, Gareyev says, "I think the US can have an impact on Afghanistan as a base for terrorism but it won't be able to liquidate all the terrorists." Bombing is not enough to fight terrorism, says the general, the root of evil needs to be eradicated. Terrorism is big business, with drug production in Afghanistan alone raking in millions of dollars, much of which goes to Osama bin Laden.[2] So tackling terrorism entails locating the sources and organisers of the drug trade.

"I think the US can have an impact on Afghanistan as a base for terrorism but it won't be able to liquidate all the terrorists."

The problem also lies in people's perception of US ideology: many believe it wants to enhance its prosperity at the expense of other countries, and to some extent, this is responsible for terrorism, surmises Gareyev.

The country's unilateral military action is also a cause for concern among several nations, says Moiseyev. While Russia condemned the NATO aggression against Yugoslavia, it is supporting the US operations against the terrorist bases in Afghanistan. In 10 years of post-Soviet history, Russia has not conducted any military operations abroad except for peacekeeping missions in the Balkans, Sierra Leone and the CIS [Commonwealth Independent States—consisting of Russia and several eastern European and central Asian states]. "But these operations were all

---

2. the Saudi national who founded the al Qaeda terrorist organization

planned and implemented by the UN and the collective decision-making bodies of the CIS," says Moiseyev. "Russia only implemented their decisions. The US, on the other hand, sometimes plans military campaigns and acts as it sees fit. This causes concern in the world community."

Moiseyev, however, is all for supporting forces opposed to the current regime in Kabul [Afghanistan's capital city]. "I think the US and Russia should actively support the anti-Taliban forces to help them clear the country of religious fanatics."

The nature of impact that such an exercise will have on Afghanistan is a matter of speculation. But "history shows that any attempts to establish a strong central power in Afghanistan end in failure," says Gareyev. The Tajiks and Uzbeks should have a certain degree of autonomy with the Pashtoons taking the leading role, he believes. "I don't think we will see an ethnic group trying to secede because this would mean the war will never end. The Pashtoons won't let Afghanistan be carved." In his book *The Afghan Harvest*, he quotes [economist Friedrich] Engels, who said of the Afghans: "Only their unbridled hatred of state power and their love of personal independence prevents them from becoming a powerful nation."

Despite this, says Sudjayev, "No one can beat the Afghans." And the longer the war continues against the Taliban, the fewer allies America will have left in Afghanistan, he adds. Perhaps America should pay heed. Ten years, after all, is a long time to learn lessons in defeat.

4

The United States Must Pursue Regime Change in Afghanistan

Charles Krauthammer

Before the U.S.-led war in Afghanistan was launched, many people debated what the goals of the war should be. Some believed that the goal of military action should be to destroy the al Qaeda terrorist network, while others felt that the war should fundamentally change the Afghan nation by toppling the ruling Taliban regime and replacing it with a Western-style democracy. Charles Krauthammer, Pulitzer Prize–winning columnist for the *Washington Post*, argues in the following piece that the goal of the Afghan war should not be simply to pursue Osama bin Laden and the terrorists behind the September 11, 2001, attacks. Instead, he says that the United States must remove the Taliban regime entirely. He states that the goal of the war on terror is to end regimes that support terrorist goals, starting with the Taliban.

Yes, we need to get Osama bin Laden. Yes, we need to bring down the terrorist networks. But the overriding aim of the war on terrorism is changing regimes. And it starts with the Taliban.

Searching Afghan caves for bin Laden is precisely the trap he would wish us to fall into. Terrorists cannot operate without the succor and protection of governments. The planet is divided into countries. Unless terrorists want to

Charles Krauthammer, "The War: A Road Map," *The Washington Post*, September 28, 2001. Copyright © 2001 by The Washington Post Book World Service/ Washington Post Writers Group. Reproduced by permission of the author.

camp in Antarctica, they must live in sovereign states. The objective of this war must be to make it impossible or intolerable for any state to harbor, protect or aid and abet terrorists. The point is not to swat every mosquito but to drain the swamp.

Make an Example of the Taliban

The war begins in Afghanistan. The first objective must be to destroy the Taliban regime. Indeed, to make an example of the Taliban, to show the world—and especially regimes engaged in terrorism—that President Bush was serious when he told the nation that we make no distinction between the terrorists and the governments that harbor them. The take-home lesson must be: Harbor terrorists—and your regime dies.

The objective of this war must be to make it impossible or intolerable for any state to harbor, protect or aid and abet terrorists.

Remember the context. Radical Islam is riding a wave of victories: The bombing of the Marine barracks in 1983 that drove the United States out of Lebanon; the killing of 18 American soldiers in Mogadishu in 1993 that drove the United States out of Somalia; and, in between, the war that drove the other superpower, the Soviet Union, out of Afghanistan [in the 1980s].

And now Sept. 11, which sent America into shock and leaves it deep in fear. Victory breeds victory. The terrorists feel invincible, and those sitting on the fence in the region are waiting to see whether they really are. Overthrowing the Taliban would reverse the historical tide and profoundly affect the psychological balance of power.

The United States Must Stand Firm

This step is so obvious and necessary that it is deeply troubling to see the secretary of state begin to wobble. If the Taliban give up bin Laden and al Qaeda (his terrorist network), said [U.S. secretary of state Colin] Powell on [September 25, 2001], "we wouldn't be worrying about whether they are the regime in power or not." He then offered carrots ("significant benefits . . . a better relationship with the West") and even hinted at American aid.

Carrots? Aid? After Sept. 11? The Taliban share responsibility for the worst mass murder in American history. For that they must be made to pay, or what meaning is there to the president's pledge that "justice will be done"?

If the administration goes wobbly on the Taliban, it might as well give up the war on terrorism before it starts. The Taliban are dripping blood. They are totally isolated. They are militarily vulnerable. On the ground they face a fierce armed opposition, the Northern Alliance, that is ready and eager to take Kabul. With our support, it could.

It may not be easy and it may not be quick. But such a signal victory is essential.

Chapter 2

Assessing the War and Its Outcomes

1

The U.S. Attack on Afghanistan Is Unethical

William Norman Grigg and Jennifer A. Gritt

As Afghan civilian casualties mounted in Afghanistan in late 2001, it became increasingly difficult for many writers and activists across the political spectrum to view the U.S.-led attack as just. In the next selection conservative journalist and senior editor of the *New American* magazine, William Norman Grigg, and peace activist Jennifer A. Gritt assert that the U.S.-led war in Afghanistan is unethical. The claim that the United States is fighting a just, defensive war in Afghanistan is false, they argue, because the United States is bombing heavily populated areas of Afghanistan knowing that many innocent civilians, as well as the hiding terrorists, will be killed. This practice violates the historic standards of Just War and the Western values that the United States seeks to defend.

Within hours of the terrorist attack upon our country, President George W. Bush promised that those responsible for that atrocity would be brought to justice. He also warned, "We will make no distinction between the terrorists who committed these acts and those who harbor them." This warning was directed primarily at the Taliban regime then controlling Afghanistan, where Osama bin Laden had set up his base and training camps.

Under what the Constitution refers to as the "law of nations," a government sheltering and supporting terrorists is implicated in their despicable acts. But using military force

William Norman Grigg and Jennifer A. Gritt, "Indiscriminate Warfare," *The New American*, vol. 18, February 25, 2002, p. 29. Copyright © 2002 by American Opinion Publishing, Inc. Reproduced by permission.

to root out bin Laden and his minions faced both practical and moral obstacles. As the September 24th 2001 issue of *Newsweek* noted, bin Laden's terrorist infrastructure in Afghanistan presented a very challenging target. "If the goal is to coerce the Taliban into handing him over, the prospects are . . . bleak," reported the journal. "Afghanistan's shattered rural economy has almost no targets vulnerable to airstrikes, which would mainly make a lot of rubble jump."

Within the Afghan "rubble" could be found many innocent noncombatants who, unlike bin Laden's terrorist cadres, couldn't protect themselves from airstrikes. The most accessible Afghan targets for military action were a few scattered training camps, cities, and villages, as well as the Tora Bora cave complex. However, those targets were located either within, or in proximity to, civilian population centers, making it difficult at best for a military campaign against Afghanistan to comply with the "Just War" principle of "discrimination" between belligerents and noncombatants.

> *There is ample cause to believe that the bombing campaign . . . was hardly the antiseptic exercise that the Bush administration insists.*

Compounding this difficulty was the logistical challenge of conducting missile strikes and bombing attacks against land-locked targets from thousands of miles away, and the use of the Northern Alliance—a motley assortment of tribal warriors—as ground-based surrogates for the U.S.-led assault.

Questionable Results

According to the Bush administration and much of the major media, the military campaign against the Taliban and bin Laden's Afghan network was entirely successful and miraculously free of "collateral damage" to innocent civilians. But bin Laden and his top leaders are still at large, and substantial numbers of Taliban fighters continue to put up armed resistance across the Afghan countryside. This suggests that declaring victory is premature.

Furthermore, there is ample cause to believe that the bombing campaign, which employed some of the largest non-nuclear bombs in the U.S. arsenal, was hardly the antiseptic exercise that the Bush administration insists. In fact, official statements from administration officials, especially Secretary of Defense Donald Rumsfeld, indicate that discriminating between combatants and civilians was not a compelling priority.

Evidence emerged that some of the dead pro-Taliban prisoners had their arms tied behind their backs.

Of course, civilian casualties tragically occur in any war, even those fought responsibly on behalf of the most righteous causes. With thousands of Americans dead from murderous attacks on our nation, a military response against those who perpetrated those attacks is entirely appropriate—assuming that it is carried out morally and under the proper authority. . . .

The war on Afghanistan has not been carried out in harmony with the Just War concept of "war decision law," requiring that the proper public authority (in our case, the U.S. Congress) must make the decision to commit a nation to war. We must now examine whether the campaign satisfies the "war conduct law" of the Just War doctrine.[1]

Responsibility for Casualties

"We did not start this war," observed Secretary Rumsfeld at a Defense Department news briefing. "So understand, responsibility for every single casualty in this war, whether they're innocent Afghans or innocent Americans, rests at the feet of the Al Qaeda and the Taliban."

Rumsfeld's statement is impossible to reconcile with the "war conduct law," under which those who fight just defensive wars are morally responsible for avoidable civilian deaths. The logic of the terrorist, however, justifies indiscriminate use of lethal violence because of the supposed righteousness of the cause—and the "responsibility" for in-

1. The Just War doctrine states that all of the following conditions must be met for a war to be considered legitimate use of force: The damage inflicted by the aggressor on the nation or community of nations must be lasting, grave, and certain. All other means of putting an end to it must have been shown to be impractical or ineffective. There must be serious prospects of success. The use of arms must not produce evils and disorders graver than the evil to be eliminated. The power of modern means of destruction weighs very heavily in evaluating this condition.

nocent people dying supposedly rests with those who do not submit to terrorist demands. Obviously, there is no moral equivalence between Osama bin Laden's motives and the stated objectives of the "war on terrorism"; thus it is more than a little unsettling to see Secretary Rumsfeld embracing a moral standard of war conduct similar to bin Laden's.

Possible War Crimes Committed by the United States

Secretary Rumsfeld also made unsettling comments regarding the treatment of hostile Afghans attempting to surrender. Referring to the [battle in the northern Afghan city of] Mazar-e-Sharif in which some 500 pro-Taliban fighters were killed, Rumsfeld was quoted as saying that "no quarter" would be given to troops trying to surrender.

"The United States is not inclined to negotiate surrenders," stated Rumsfeld in a November 9th [2001] press briefing, insisting that the anti-Taliban Northern Alliance was in a better position to negotiate. "If people try to [surrender], we are declining. That is not what we're there to do, is to begin accepting prisoners and impounding them in some way or making judgments."

According to the official account, most of the killings at Mazar-e-Sharif were carried out by the Northern Alliance, with support and guidance from U.S. forces, for the purpose of putting down a prisoner uprising. Under time-honored laws governing warfare, armed prisoner revolt can be put down with severity. However, after the dust settled around the prison fortress and Red Cross workers were allowed to remove the bodies, evidence emerged that some of the dead pro-Taliban prisoners had their arms tied behind their backs.

Whether carried out by U.S. forces or our allies, summary execution of prisoners would seriously violate the Geneva Convention [which governed international law for conducting war]. Just as importantly, it would violate our nation's long established moral traditions in warfare. [World War II] general George S. Patton, an exemplar of that tradition, urged his soldiers: "Kill all the Germans you can, but do not put them up against a wall and kill them. Do your killing while they are still fighting. After a man has surrendered, he should be treated exactly in accordance with the Rules of Land Warfare, and just as you would hope to be treated if you were foolish enough to surrender. Americans do not kick people in the teeth after they are down."

Serious questions were also raised about a December 1st [2001] U.S. bombing raid that destroyed villages outside Kabul. Over 100 civilians were reportedly killed in the village of Kama Ado, despite residents insisting that no al-Qaeda terrorists were ever there. The December 4th *Seattle Times* noted, "anti-Taliban leaders say local villagers, not terrorists, are dying in the raids because Americans are using faulty intelligence."

Concerns were also raised over the bombing of Kandahar, a city regarded as an al-Qaeda stronghold. "In Kandahar, the hope remains that Taliban and Al-Qaeda forces will surrender, but we have reason to believe that [terrorist leader Mullah] Omar may have instructed his forces to continue fighting, which of course is putting the civilian population in Kandahar and the region at risk," Rumsfeld told reporters. "Indeed, hiding in the city, the Taliban are in effect using the civilian population of Kandahar as shields." In any case, Rumsfeld assured reporters, "We know this much for certain—the United States has taken extraordinary measures to avoid civilian casualties in this campaign."

But these statements contradict each other. If the U.S. was aware that al-Qaeda fighters were hiding within a village of several hundred innocent people, bombing the village from the air would be an indiscriminate measure, producing a grossly disproportionate combatant-to-civilian death ratio. Once again, a useful ethical benchmark was offered by General Patton, who in the middle of World War II condemned "the seemingly barbaric bombardment of the centers of cities" by both Allied and Axis forces.

Assessing the Human Cost

In his study of civilian casualties in Afghanistan, University of New Hampshire Professor Marc W. Herold observes: "A legacy of the ten years of civil war during the 80s is that many military garrisons and facilities are located in urban areas where the Soviet-backed government had placed them since they could be better protected there from attacks by the rural mujahideen. Successor Afghan governments [including the Taliban] inherited these emplacements." This meant that many of the legitimate military targets of the anti-Taliban air campaign were located in the middle of urban centers.

Using figures derived from a variety of independent media and humanitarian sources, and other eyewitness accounts, Professor Herold compiled a civilian death toll of 3,767 Afghans for the first two months of the [2001 Afghan] military campaign—a figure eerily similar to the body count of those killed in the terrorist attack on the World Trade Center. "What causes the documented high level of civilian casualties . . . in the U.S. air war upon Afghanistan?" wrote Professor Herold. "The explanation is the apparent willingness of U.S. military strategists to fire missiles into, and drop bombs upon, heavily populated areas of Afghanistan."

Again, there is no moral equivalence between Osama bin Laden's motives in organizing the terrorist attack upon American civilians, and the stated objectives of the U.S.-led bombing of Afghanistan. The innocent dead in New York City and at the Pentagon were specifically targeted for the purpose of sowing terror; this is not true of the innocent civilians killed due to the Afghan bombing campaign. But if those thousands of civilians were killed as a result of our policymakers' guilty negligence, it would seriously undermine the moral stature of our anti-terrorism campaign.

There is no moral equivalence between Osama bin Laden's motives . . . and the stated objectives of the U.S.-led bombing of Afghanistan.

Why should we worry about the death of Afghan noncombatants? Aren't we entitled, because of the obvious righteousness of our cause and the precedent set in previous wars, to use drastic measures to punish the terrorists and prevent further attacks? Conservative columnist Ann Coulter certainly thinks so, and her remarks in a post-September 11th column express the views of many Americans. "We should invade their countries, kill their leaders and convert them to Christianity," wrote Coulter. "We weren't punctilious about locating and punishing only Hitler and his top officers. We carpet-bombed German cities, we killed civilians. That's war. And this is war."

As the war proceeds, predicts David Brooks of the neoconservative journal *Weekly Standard*, "We will care a lot more about ends—winning the war—than we will about means. We will debate whether it is necessary to torture prisoners who have information about biological attacks. We will destroy innocent villages by accident, shrug our shoulders, and continue fighting. In an age of conflict, bourgeois virtues like compassion, tolerance, and industriousness are valued less than the classical virtues of courage, steadfastness, and a ruthless desire for victory."

There is an ominous echo in Brooks' casual denigration of "bourgeois virtues." During World War II and the Cold War, after all, America's identified enemies were totalitarian socialist regimes that loudly condemned "bourgeois virtues" and extolled "ruthlessness." The Bush administration and its media surrogates tirelessly warn that bin Laden and his comrades are seeking to destroy Western civilization—but if we cast aside the moral restrictions embodied in the Christian Just War tradition, we would accomplish that diabolical task all by ourselves.

Possible Legal Ramifications of the U.S.-Led War

Because the Bush administration has chosen to conduct the "war on terrorism" as a UN-supervised campaign, our nation faces several unprecedented dangers. For example, U.S. military personnel could find themselves being investigated, or even prosecuted, by the UN for carrying out policies violating the customary rules of warfare.

In 1995, Serbian ruler Slobodan Milosevic was welcomed as a "guarantor" of the UN-administered Bosnian peace accord, despite accusations that he was guilty of war crimes in the Bosnian civil war. Four years later, NATO [North Atlantic Treaty Organization], a UN affiliate, launched a bombing campaign against Serbia that killed hundreds of civilians and wrecked much of Serbia's economic infrastructure. Early last year [2001], Milosevic was extradited to The Hague[2] to stand trial before a UN tribunal—the first time the world body has arraigned a former head of state for prosecution. Significantly, the indictment against Milosevic includes charges relating to his conduct before 1995—atrocities for which he was allegedly responsible before the "international community" embraced him as a "peacemaker."

---

2. the home of the International Criminal Court in the Netherlands

Is it unreasonable to believe that if the empowerment of the UN and its judicial organs proceeds apace, U.S. military leaders and policymakers might someday face arraignment for alleged war crimes in Afghanistan, and in other battlefields of the "war on terrorism"? Significantly, Carla Del Ponte, chief prosecutor for the UN tribunal in The Hague, investigated charges that U.S. pilots committed war crimes during the NATO bombing of Serbia. And UN Human Rights Commissioner Mary Robinson has suggested that the treatment of captured Afghan fighters at Camp X-Ray [the U.S. internment camp for terrorists], in Guantanamo Bay, Cuba, may violate UN "human rights" standards. (Typical of the UN, Robinson has not uttered a syllable of condemnation for Fidel Castro's gulags, which have operated for decades on the same island.)

Our present course combines two of the worst alternatives: It undermines the historic Just War standards that help define us as a society, while fortifying the UN's spurious system of "international law." The potential damage if we persist in this course would easily eclipse anything that bin Laden's minions could inflict upon us.

2

America Is Losing the War in Afghanistan

Osama bin Laden

In this sermon, broadcast on the Arabic al Jazeera network in early February 2003, al Qaeda leader Osama bin Laden outlines his reasons for planning the September 11, 2001, terror attacks and claims that the United States has not been able to achieve its goals in the subsequent war in Afghanistan. He says that America was attacked because it oppresses the Muslim world and that now the myth of American power has been destroyed. The mujahideen, or holy warriors, are winning the jihad in Afghanistan, says bin Laden, because the United States misunderstands the nature of the conflict there, just as it cannot comprehend the reasons behind the September 11 attacks. Bin Laden calls for an expanded holy war, citing September 11 and what he considers the United States' unsuccessful war in Afghanistan as proof of the West's vulnerability.

The gang of black-hearted criminals in the White House was misrepresenting the [reasons for the September 11, 2001, attacks] and that their leader [President Bush], who is a fool whom all obey, was claiming that we were jealous of their way of life, while the truth—which the Pharaoh of our generation conceals—is that we strike at them because of the way they oppress us in the Muslim world, especially in Palestine and Iraq, and because of their occupation of the Land of the Two Holy Places. When the *Mujahideen* saw this they decided to act in secret and to move the battle right into his

Osama bin Laden, sermon delivered on the Feast of Sacrifice, February 11, 2003.

[the U.S. president's] country and his own territory.

On that blessed Tuesday, the 23rd of *jumada al-thani*, 1422 [in the Muslim calendar], which corresponds to September 11th, 2001, while the Zio [Israeli]-American alliance was still using American tanks and planes and Jewish hands to reap [the lives] of our sons and our people in the land of al-Aqsa [Palestine], while our sons in Iraq were dying as a result of the oppression of the unjust siege [inflicted on them] by America and her agents; and while the Muslim world was still very far from genuinely supporting Islam; while things were in this state of frustration, desperation and procrastination—on the part of the Muslims, with the exception of those on whom Allah had had mercy,—and a state of injustice, arrogance and aggression—on the part of the Zio-American alliance; and while the land of Uncle Sam, heedless in its transgressions, bellowing its tyranny, 'puffed up its cheeks in contempt of the people and strutted merrily on the face of the earth,'[1] without paying heed to anyone, believing that nothing could harm it—then disaster struck them.

People discovered that it was possible to strike at America, that oppressive power, and that it was possible to humiliate it.

Come let me tell you what that terrible disaster means: the 'unkempt of hair and dusty of foot' pounced—they who are everywhere hunted down, young men who believed in their Lord, whom Allah had guided to the right path, whose hearts He had strengthened and filled with faith. [These young men, when it comes to acting] for Allah's cause, do not fear 'the reprimands of those who seek to find fault' because they desire only Allah's recompense; their hearts do not allow them to close to injustice; they sacrifice their lives, but never their honor.

They carried out the raid by means of enemy planes in a courageous and splendid operation the like of which mankind had never before witnessed. They smashed the American idols and damaged its very heart, the Pentagon. They struck the very heart of the American economy, rubbed America's nose in the dirt and dragged its pride through the

---

1. Osama bin Laden quotes often from the Koran.

mud. The towers of New York collapsed, and their collapse precipitated an even greater debacle: the collapse of the myth of America the great power and the collapse of the myth of democracy; people began to understand that American values could sink no lower. The myth of the land of freedom was destroyed, the myth of American National security was smashed and the myth of the CIA collapsed, all praise and thanks to Allah.

Western Contempt for Muslims

One of the most important positive results of the raids on New York and Washington was the revelation of the truth regarding the conflict between the Crusaders [the West] and the Muslims. [The raids] revealed the strength of the hatred which the Crusaders feel towards us, as the two raids peeled the lamb's skin off the back of the American wolf and revealed the hideous truth. The whole world awoke from its slumber, and the Muslims were alerted to the importance of the [Muslim] principle which states that positions of alliance or hostility may be taken [only] for the sake of Allah. The spirit of religious brotherhood among Muslims was likewise strengthened, which constitutes a great step forward along the road towards uniting Muslims under the banner of monotheism in order to establish the rightly-guided Caliphate [or Muslim rulership], God willing. People discovered that it was possible to strike at America, that oppressive power, and that it was possible to humiliate it, to bring it into contempt and to defeat it. For the first time, the majority of the American people [now] understand the truth of the Palestinian issue and that what hit them in Manhattan is a result of the oppressive policy of their government.

To sum up: America is a great power possessed of tremendous military might and a wide-ranging economy, but all this is built upon an unstable foundation which can be targeted, with special attention to its obvious weak spots. If it [America] is hit in one hundredth of those spots, God willing, it will stumble, wither away and relinquish world leadership and its oppression.

A small group of young Islamic [fighters] managed, despite the international alliance drawn up against them, to provide people with [concrete] proof of the fact that it is possible to wage war upon and fight against a so-called 'great power.' They managed to protect their religion and effectively to serve the objectives of their Nation [of Islam] better than the governments and peoples of the fifty-odd countries of the Muslim world, because they used *Jihad* as a means to defend their faith. As Abu Hifala [poet and dean at Al Hussein University in Ma'an, Jordan] said: 'Victory has its reasons, as does defeat, and any means which brings victory is worthwhile; the paths which lead to exalted ends are different, and the shortest of them is that which sheds blood and which has noble people [standing] at both its sides.'

The Fighting in Afghanistan

I am happy to tell you that the Jihad in Afghanistan is going well, thank God, and that things are improving in favor of the *Mujahideen*, thanks to Allah. We are now in the second year of fighting [2003], and America has not managed to accomplish its objectives; on the contrary, it has become embroiled in the Afghan swamp. What America regarded in the first months [of the war] as a victory, after it took control of the cities evacuated by the *Mujahideen* [has turned out to be something quite different]. Military experts in general, and those familiar with Afghanistan in particular, know that this was a tactical withdrawal, which suited the nature of the Taliban state and the nature of the Afghans who have a long history of guerrilla warfare. The Taliban state had no regular army to defend the cities. Therefore, the Afghans relied—after placing their trust in Allah—on their [greatest] strength, namely, their ability to conduct guerrilla warfare from the depths of their impassable mountains, using the same tactics with which, thanks to Allah, they had previously defeated the Soviet army. This became an established fact after the guerrilla operations began, and their number has now reached an average of two operations per day. The Americans are now in real trouble: they are unable to defend their own forces, nor can they establish a state capable of protecting its own president—let alone anyone else.

The Americans are now in real trouble: they are unable to defend their own forces.

By the grace of Allah, coordination among all the *Mujahideen* has been achieved in the past year, and all engage enthusiastically in *Jihad* and consider it a duty. If their means were not so limited, they could increase the number of daily operations to that of their earlier *Jihad* against the Russians, and which the Americans would not be able to endure. Hence it is incumbent on the [Islamic] Nation today to support *Jihad* in general, and [specifically] in Palestine and Afghanistan. These pivotal [areas] are highly important, and we should focus on them, so as to exhaust the Jews, who are the Americans' allies, and so as to exhaust the Americans, who are allied with the Jews. America's defeat in Afghanistan will be, God willing, the beginning of its end.

You should know that seeking to kill Americans and Jews everywhere in the world is one of the greatest duties [for Muslims].

You shall suffer no harm from us [al Qaeda] nor from our brethren the Afghan *Mujahideen*, God willing. We hope that we shall suffer no harm from you. The [Islamic] Nation is now facing a battle for Allah, in which there should be no display of either weakness or evil-doing. The forces of the Muslims will gather against the forces of the infidels. Now is the time to repent of sins and transgressions. It is likewise incumbent upon the Nation, now that it's facing this crucial issue—which is very serious and no joking matter—to give up a life of fun and enjoyment, extravagance and luxury. It [the Islamic Nation] should toughen itself and prepare itself for real life, a life of killing and war, of shooting and hand-to-hand combat. Here is what Sheikh al-Islam [a very famous Muslim scholar] said with regard to a situation of internal conflict similar to the one in which we find ourselves. He said: 'You should know, may Allah render you successful, that, according to an authentic tradition transmitted from the Prophet by many chains [of transmitters], [the Prophet] said: 'There will always be within my Nation a group which knows the truth, who are not affected by whosoever abandons them or opposes them until the Day of Judgment.'

In this *fitna* [internal strife] people have split into three groups: [1] those who will triumph with Allah's help, i.e., those who are waging *Jihad* against the [aforementioned] corrupt people. [2] The disobedient, i.e., those [corrupt] people [whom we have just mentioned] and those who joined them from among the feeble-minded so-called Muslims. [3] The laggards, i.e., those who refrain from joining the *Jihad*, even though they are true Muslims. Let every one [of you] examine whether he belongs to the 'triumphant group,' the 'laggards' or the 'disobedient group,' for there is no fourth one.

He, may Allah have mercy on him, also said: By Allah, if the early Muslims from among the *Muhajirun* [those who emigrated with Muhammad from Mecca to Medina] and the *ansar* [Muhammad's early supporters in Medina], such as Abu Bakr, 'Umar, 'Uthman, 'Ali and others, were alive today, they would regard fighting against those criminals as one of the most virtuous acts. Only he who miscalculates will allow himself to miss such a battle; [by refraining] he makes a fool of himself and is deprived of immense reward in this life and in the hereafter.

I instruct the young people to exert every effort in *Jihad*, for it is they upon whom this duty primarily devolves, as was indicated by al-Shatibi in his [book] *al-Muwafaqat*.

You should know that seeking to kill Americans and Jews everywhere in the world is one of the greatest duties [for Muslims], and the good deed most preferred by Allah, the Exalted.

I also bid them [the young people] to rally round the honest *'ulama* [religious scholars] and the sincere preachers, that is, those who practice what they teach; I also counsel them to manage their affairs in secrecy, especially the military affairs of *Jihad*.

I am happy to inform all of you—and our brothers in Palestine in particular—that your brethren who are engaged in *Jihad* continue to pursue the way of *Jihad*, targeting the Jews and the Americans. We shall never abandon you. Go on, continue the fighting with Allah's blessing, and we too, with you, will continue to fight, God willing.

Before concluding, I urge myself, as I urge my Muslim brethren to set their faces towards *Jihad*, for the sake of Allah, with the words of the poet [al-Timmals ibu al-Hakim al-Ta'i]:

> I am leading my horse and casting him and myself this year into one of the battles
>
> O Lord, when death arrives, let it not be upon a bier covered with green shrouds

Rather, let my grave be in the belly of a vulture, tranquil in the sky, among hovering vultures

I shall be martyr resting among a group of young men whom death will overtake in a terrible ravine

Horsemen of [the tribe of] Shayban, whom piety united, brave warriors alighting from their mounts [to fight face to face] when the two armies advance to meet each other

When they leave this world they will leave behind suffering and attain that which is promised in the Koran

Finally, I instruct myself and my Muslim brethren to fear God both privately and publicly, and to implore Allah and beseech him to accept our repentance and relieve us of our distress.

O Lord, give us your blessing in this world and in the next, and protect us from the fires of Hell.

We beseech Allah to free our captives from the hands of the Americans and their accomplices—foremost among them Sheikh 'Umar ibn 'Abd al-Rahman and Sheikh Sa'id ibn Zu'eyr and our brethren in Guantanamo [U.S. detention camp in Cuba]—and to strengthen the *Mujahideen* in Palestine and other Muslim lands. May they be victorious, and may He help us triumph over our enemy.

I also bid you, as I bid myself, to keep the name of Allah on your lips, to read the Koran often, and to ponder it, for it contains counsel from your Lord and healing for the heart, and guidance and mercy for the Muslims. Allah is all-powerful, but most people do not understand.

Our final word is: praise be to Allah, Lord of the universe.

3

Afghanistan Is an Important Success in the War on Terror

Donald H. Rumsfeld

The rapid collapse of the Taliban following the U.S.-led attack on Afghanistan was a major victory in the war on terror. As of July 2002, al Qaeda had lost its central base of operations in Afghanistan and a provisional Afghan authority had begun reconstruction efforts with the help of an international coalition. In the following extract of his testimony to the U.S. Senate Armed Services Committee, in July 2002, Secretary of State Donald H. Rumsfeld argues that with U.S. and coalition assistance, Afghanistan is on its way to becoming a stable, independent state. He maintains that the human rights violations that characterized the Taliban's rule have decreased and that the Afghans' terrible living conditions vastly improved since the war began. Those changes not only point to a hopeful future for Afghanistan, he asserts, but also provide a sound basis for continuing the global campaign against terror.

While we have made good progress in a relatively short period of time, let there be no doubt: this war is far from over. The road ahead will be difficult and dangerous. We face determined adversaries. They have demonstrated ingenuity and a callous disregard for innocent human life. Victory will not come easily or quickly—it will require patience from Americans at home, and the courage of our ser-

Donald H. Rumsfeld, testimony before the Senate Armed Services Committee on Progress in Afghanistan, Washington, DC, July 31, 2002.

vice men and women abroad. Fortunately, patience and courage are virtues our nation has in abundance. And I have no doubt that we will prevail.

Last fall [2001], when President Bush announced the start of the war on terrorism, he declared war not just on the perpetrators of the deadly attacks of September 11th [2001], but against all terrorists of global reach, their organizations and sponsors.

Terrorists that threaten us will find no safe haven, no sanctuary, anywhere.

He made clear his determination that terrorists that threaten us will find no safe haven, no sanctuary, anywhere—and that their state sponsors will be held accountable, and made to understand there is a heavy price to be paid for financing, harboring, or otherwise supporting terrorists. And he issued a worldwide call to arms, inviting all freedom-loving nations to join us in this fight.

In the intervening months, the world has responded to the President's call. The global coalition President Bush assembled comprises some 70 nations. They are helping in many different ways. Most are sharing intelligence. Many are seizing terrorist assets or breaking up terrorist cells on their territory. Others are providing airlift, basing, over-flight and refueling, or are contributing air, sea and ground forces, combat air patrols, mine clearing and special operations. Some are helping quietly, others openly. But each is making important contributions to the global war on terror.

We are now roughly nine months into this war—still closer to the beginning than to the end. But while much difficult work remains before us, it is worth taking a moment to reflect and take stock of just how much U.S. and coalition forces have accomplished thus far in reversing the tide of terrorism.

Afghan Conditions Before U.S. Intervention

At this time last year [2001], Afghanistan was a pariah state. The Taliban regime was in power and brutally repressed the Afghan people. The country was a sanctuary for thousands of foreign terrorists, who had free range to train, plan and organize attacks on innocent civilians across the globe. There was harsh repressive rule. The economy and banking sector were in a state of collapse, and the country was financially dependent on terrorist networks and overseas Islamic extremist elements. A humanitarian crisis of considerable proportions loomed. Humanitarian assistance was disrupted, famine was pervasive, and refugees were fleeing the country by the hundreds of thousands.

Consider just some of the human rights reports which detailed conditions in Afghanistan before the arrival of coalition forces:

According to the State Department's February 2001 Human Rights Report, "The Taliban continued to commit numerous, serious and systemic abuses. Citizens were unable to change their government or choose their leaders peacefully. The Taliban carried out summary justice . . . and . . . were responsible for political and other extra-judicial killings, including targeted killings, summary executions, and deaths in custody. . . . Women and girls were subjected to rape, kidnapping, and forced marriage."

Afghanistan is no longer a base of global terrorist operations or a breeding ground for radical Islamic militancy.

Amnesty International's 2001 human rights report declared that Afghans suffered pervasive "human rights abuses, including arbitrary detention and torture. . . . The *Taliban* continued to impose harsh restrictions on personal conduct and behavior as a means of enforcing their particular interpretation of Islamic law. . . . Young women living in areas captured by the *Taliban* . . . were reportedly abducted by guards and taken against their will as 'wives' for *Taliban* commanders."

Human Rights Watch's report for 2001 described a situation where "Taliban forces subjected local civilians to a ruthless and systematic policy of collective punishment. Summary executions, the deliberate destruction of homes, and confiscation of farmland were recurrent practices in these campaigns." There was "systematic discrimination against women. . . . Violations of the dress code . . . could result in public beatings and lashing by the Religious Police, who wielded leather batons reinforced with metal studs. Women were not permitted to work outside the home except in the area of health care, and girls over eight years old were not permitted to attend school. The decrees contributed to an illiteracy level for women of over 90 percent." And all of this enforced by the so-called Minister for the Promotion of Virtue and the Prevention of Vice.

Human Rights Watch also reported widespread "harassment of international aid agency staff," who were in some cases taken hostage. According to the State Department report, in August 2001 "the Taliban arrested eight foreign aid workers affiliated with an NGO [nongovernmental organization] on charges of proselytizing. An estimated 48 Afghan employees of the NGO also were arrested and reportedly also charged with apostasy. . . . The Taliban reportedly stated that 59 children who had been taught by the arrested workers were sent to a correctional facility."

What a Difference a Year Makes

Today [2002], thanks to coalition efforts—and the remarkable courage of our men and women in uniform—the Taliban have been driven from power, al Qaeda is on the run, Afghanistan is no longer a base of global terrorist operations or a breeding ground for radical Islamic militancy, the beatings by religious police and executions in soccer stadiums have stopped, the humanitarian crisis has been averted, international workers are no longer held hostage, aid is once again flowing, and the Afghan people have been liberated. Afghanistan is a free nation, where aid workers can provide humanitarian aid, girls can study, women can work, the people can choose their leaders peacefully and refugees can return.

Grand Assembly

Through the recent Loya Jirga process, the Afghan people have exercised their right of self-determination. More than 1,500 delegates from all 32 provinces and all ethnic backgrounds came together under one roof to chart their nation's political future. A new president has been selected, a new cabinet has been sworn in, a transitional government representative of the Afghan people has been established to lead the nation [through 2004], until a constitutional Loya Jirga is held.

The new Afghan government is still in its early stages, and it doesn't yet have the institutions of government to direct, such as internal security, tax collection and the like. But it has begun the process of working to develop the banking sector, tax laws, and a new currency. New trade and commercial investment policies are also being put in place, with the aim of building foreign investor confidence. A corps of civil servants is being established, with pay under UN supervision, and ministries are beginning to function. The judicial system is being reformed, so that rule of law can take root. A growing civil society is emerging, with open political discourse and an emerging free press. We're fortunate that their leadership is taking seriously the challenge of self-government.

Military and Humanitarian Projects

With self-government must eventually come self-sufficiency —and that self-sufficiency must, over time, also extend to security. That is why we are working with the new Afghan government to lay the foundations for longer-term stability and to reverse the conditions that allowed terrorist regimes to take root in the first place. The U.S. and others are helping to train a new Afghan National Army—a force committed not to one group or faction but to the defense of the en-

New recruits of the Afghan National Army practice saluting at a training site in Kabul in May 2002.

tire nation, which we hope will allow Afghans to take responsibility for their own security rather than relying on foreign forces. [In late July 2002] the 1st Battalion of more than 300 soldiers graduated—and there are an additional 600 Afghan soldiers being trained in two battalions. In all, we expect to train 18 battalions—over 10,000 soldiers—by the end of 2003. We are also "training the trainers" so that the process can eventually become self-sustaining. Already some 38 countries have offered weapons, equipment, funds or support for this effort.

We have also helped to avert a humanitarian catastrophe in Afghanistan. The U.S. and coalition partners have delivered over 500,000 metric tons of food since the start of the war—enough to feed almost 7 million needy Afghans. Thanks to those efforts, the grim predictions of starvation last winter [2002] did not come to pass. Today, the United States is providing over $450 million in humanitarian assistance for the Afghan people.

Today, the United States is providing over $450 million in humanitarian assistance for the Afghan people.

The Department of Defense has allotted $10 million to dozens of humanitarian projects throughout Afghanistan. U.S. military civil affairs teams have dug wells, built hospitals, repaired roads, bridges and irrigation canals. We have rebuilt 49 schools in eight different regions. Thanks to those efforts, some 30,000 boys and girls—the hope and future of Afghanistan—are back in school. One civil affairs team has even introduced Afghan kids to Little League baseball. They organized two teams, which have been practicing twice a week for the past several weeks using donated baseball supplies. [In July of 2002] they held Afghanistan's first Little League game.

It must be emphasized that coalition partners are making important contributions. De-mining teams from Norway, Britain, Poland and Jordan have helped clear land mines from hundreds of thousands of square meters of terrain, although there are still an enormous number of land mines in that country. Jordan built a hospital in Mazar-e Sharif that has now treated more than 92,000 patients, including 22,000 children. Spain and Korea have also built hospitals, and Japan has pledged $500 million to rehabilitate Afghanistan. Russia has cleared out and rebuilt the Salang Tunnel, the main artery linking Kabul with the North, allowing transportation of thousands of tons of food, medicine and supplies.

Progress in the War on Terror

With the cooperation of over 90 countries, some 2,400 individuals around the world have been detained and interviewed, and over 500 enemy combatants are currently under DoD [Department of Defense] control. They are being interrogated, and are yielding information that is helping to prevent further violence and bloodshed.

For example, with the help of our Pakistani allies, we captured a senior al-Qaeda leader, Abu Zubaydah, who in turn provided information that led to the capture of others such as Jose Padilla—an American al-Qaeda operative.

Al-Qaeda forces left behind valuable intelligence information—computer hard drives, diskettes, laptops, videos, notebooks with information that has given us insight into their capabilities, how they operate, and in some cases actionable intelligence about planned terrorist operations. For example, videotapes found in an al-Qaeda safe house in Afghanistan revealed detailed plans of a plot to strike U.S. targets in Singapore. Working with Singapore authorities, that al-Qaeda cell was broken up and their planned attack disrupted.

Our goal in Afghanistan is to ensure that that country does not, again, become a terrorist training ground.

These successes must not lull us into complacency. For every terrorist plot we discover and every terrorist cell we disrupt, there are dozens of others in the works. Al Qaeda operates not only in Afghanistan, but in more than 60 countries including the U.S. Undoubtedly, coalition efforts have made recruitment harder, planning harder, and moving between countries harder. But they have trained literally thousands of terrorists who are now at large across the globe.

These "sleeper" cells undoubtedly have plans for further attacks. They had raised a good deal of money, and they still have financial backers giving them money.

Moreover, al-Qaeda is not the only global terrorist network. And terrorist networks have growing relationships with terrorist states that harbor and finance them—and may one day share weapons of mass destruction with them. What this means is that Afghanistan is only the first stage in a long, difficult and dangerous war on terrorism.

Setting and Achieving Goals

Our goal in Afghanistan is to ensure that that country does not, again, become a terrorist training ground. That work is, of course, by no means complete. Taliban and al Qaeda fugitives are still at large. Some are in Afghanistan, others fled across the borders waiting the opportunity to return. They continue to pose a threat. In recent weeks, coalition forces have come under attack again in Kandahar and Oruzgan, and Pakistani forces have engaged al Qaeda in a number of firefights, reminders of the dangers that continue to exist.

Moreover, there are still ethnic tensions within Afghanistan, and Afghanistan is still highly dependent on foreign assistance—both financial aid and humanitarian relief. The country lacks agricultural self-sufficiency, there are periodic outbreaks of cholera and dysentery, and a high infant mortality rate due to poor hygiene and inadequate medical services.

These are real challenges. But two things should be clear: One, Afghanistan is clearly a much better place to live today than it was a year ago. And two, the United States and its international partners are making a maximum effort to assist Afghanistan's new government in economic, humanitarian, security, and other fields.

Afghan leaders coming to Washington all attest that the security picture in the country is sound. The Taliban have so far failed to mount their often-predicted spring offensive. Despite numerous threats, the Loya Jirga convened with no serious security incidents. And conflicts among regional commanders have been dampened—often by discreet U.S. influence exerted by our personnel. The security situation, while not ideal, is significantly improved from what we found on our arrival [in October 2001] when the Taliban controlled and oppressed 90% of the country.

The best measure of progress is the flow of people. Before the war began, thousands upon thousands of refugees and internally displaced persons had fled their homes to escape Taliban repression. Since January [2002], hundreds of thousands of Afghan refugees and internally displaced persons have returned to their homes. The Afghan people are voting with their feet. They're coming back to their homes. That is a ringing vote of confidence in the progress that's being made in Afghanistan.

With the removal of the Taliban regime, and the efforts to break up large pockets of al-Qaeda as they tried to regroup, coalition efforts in Afghanistan are now focused mostly on smaller operations—cave-by-cave searches, sweeps for arms, intelligence, and smaller pockets of terrorists as they have dispersed. Indeed, the humanitarian effort I have described has been of invaluable assistance to us in these operations.

In most of the country coalition forces have been welcomed as liberators.

By making clear from the beginning that this was not a war against Islam, by keeping our footprint modest and partnering with Afghan forces that opposed the Taliban and al-Qaeda, and by demonstrating our concern for the welfare of the Afghan people through the delivery of humanitarian relief from the first days of the war, we showed the Afghan people that we were coming as a force of liberation, not a force of occupation.

In fact, out of 32 provinces in Afghanistan, our forces have experienced harassment attacks in only a few provinces—in the former Taliban strongholds of southern and eastern Afghanistan. In most of the country coalition forces have been welcomed as liberators.

That, in turn, has paid dividends in the hunt for Taliban and al-Qaeda. For example, we have been finding additional caches of weapons several times a week, not because we're clever or stumbled on them, but because local Afghans have come to us and told us where those caches are located. They are leading U.S. Special Forces and military personnel to those caches, so that they can be gathered up and either destroyed or provided to the new Afghan National Army. This too is a vote of confidence in coalition efforts.

The International Military Effort

Understandably, as our military mission has changed and evolved, some forces are now rotating out of Afghanistan, including from the U.K. and Canada—even as they continue to play a critical role elsewhere in the world. This should not be taken as a sign that the effort in Afghanistan is wrapping up. To the contrary [as of July 2002]:

- Turkey has increased its Afghan presence, sending over 1,300 troops to Kabul to assume leadership of the International Security Assistance Force.

- Norway, Denmark and the Netherlands will soon deploy F-16 fighters to Kyrgyzstan for air operations over Afghanistan.

- Romania has deployed an infantry battalion to Afghanistan and has offered an infantry mountain company, a nuclear, biological and chemical response company and four MiG-21 fighters, and Slovakia will soon deploy an engineering unit.

- Special Operation forces from Canada, Germany, Australia and other nations continue to work with U.S. Special Forces teams on the ground, combing through the caves, searching for Taliban and al Qaeda fugitives, gathering critical intelligence information.

Moreover, our hunt for terrorist networks is not limited to Afghanistan. At this moment, planes and ships from Australia, Bahrain, Canada, France, Germany, Greece, Italy, Japan, the Netherlands, Spain, the U.K. and others patrol the seas and skies in distant corners of the globe, conducting aerial surveillance, leadership interdiction and maritime interception operations. France and Italy have both deployed their carrier battle groups to support Operation Enduring Freedom. Germany has taken a leadership role with surface naval forces operating around the Horn of Africa. Intelligence and law enforcement agencies from dozens of countries are helping to seize terrorist assets, freeze their bank accounts, close front companies, and disrupt terrorist cells as they plan future attacks. Significant arrests have been made on many continents, from Europe to Southeast Asia.

The war on terrorism is a global campaign against a global adversary. We learned on September 11th, that in a world of international finance, communications, and transportation, even relatively isolated individuals or organizations can have global reach—and the ability to cause unprecedented destruction on innocent civilians.

The challenge for us is to find a way to live in that 21st Century world as free people. Let there be no doubt: we can do so. But it requires new ways of thinking, new ways of fighting, and new strategies for defending our people and our way of life.

In the war on terror, an enormous advantage accrues to the attacker. A terrorist can strike at any place, at any time, using any conceivable technique. And it is physically impossible to defend our people in every place, at every time, against every conceivable technique. So the only way to deal with that threat is to take the war to the terrorists—to go after them where they are, and kill them, capture them or otherwise disrupt them. As the President has said, "the first and best way to secure America's homeland is to attack the enemy where he hides and plans." This is what we have done, and are doing.

The war on terrorism began in Afghanistan, to be sure, but it will not end there. It will not end until terrorist networks have been rooted out, wherever they exist. It will not end until the state sponsors of terror are made to understand that aiding, abetting and harboring terrorists has deadly consequences for those that try it. It will not end until those developing nuclear, chemical and biological weapons end their threat to innocent men, women and children.

It will not end until our people—and the people of the world's free nations—can once again live in peace and free from fear.

4

The U.S. Victory in Afghanistan Has Improved Life for Afghan Women

Sally Armstrong

Before the U.S. attack on Afghanistan, images of Afghan women wearing head-to-toe garments called burkas and accounts of the Taliban regime's brutality toward women were widely circulated in the Western media. *Maclean's* contributing editor Sally Armstrong heard of the abuse of women's rights in Afghanistan in early 2001 and decided to visit the Afghan city of Kandahar, where she witnessed the way women's freedoms had been nearly stripped away. After the U.S.-led forces invaded Afghanistan in the wake of the September 11, 2001, terror attacks in New York and Washington, Armstrong returned to Afghanistan and found that conditions had changed radically: Women still wore the burka but they also wore high heels and makeup; they could send their daughters to school again; and they could choose their own husbands. These signs of freedom, as Armstrong explains in the next selection, are the beginning of hope for the women of Afghanistan.

In the winter of 2001, I decided to travel to Kandahar [a city in southern Afghanistan], the spiritual capital of the Taliban, to see conditions for myself. Gaining entrance to this place as a woman, a journalist and a foreigner—all red flags to the ruling Taliban—required patience and downright chicanery. I needed to invent a cover. I had learned several months earlier that Canada was funding a non-government organization called Guardians, which was doing excellent work at the Institute for Orthopedics in Kandahar. I thought there might be a match between its purposes and mine: they wanted publicity for the Institute and I wanted to report firsthand on how women were faring under the Taliban. I left Toronto armed with a visa for Pakistan, knowing I'd then have to negotiate a visa for Afghanistan. There a Taliban functionary told me the photo in my passport was not acceptable since "the woman is smiling and the yellow hair is showing." Then he announced that because I am a woman, I could only travel if accompanied by a man.

The regional director of Guardians in Afghanistan, Zalmai Mojadidi, agreed to fill the role of requisite male. At the border passport office, Mojadidi had some advice. "No say hello with your hand. Smile is okay but not so much. And no your laughing, please." We'd already had a discussion about wardrobe, and he explained that only an Afghan woman had the right to wear a burka. I wondered how it could be considered a "right" to wear a head-to-ankle body bag with a little piece of mesh in front of the eyes. We agreed that I would wear my ankle-length heavy gray winter coat, with a huge black chador wrapped around my hips, shoulders and head, which made it difficult to see, hear and walk, not to mention climb out of a truck without showing my legs.

In Kandahar the uneasy rhythms of life for Afghan women were evident everywhere, including the Institute for Orthopedics—with its Canadian flag pasted to the front wall standing out like a monument. It was modern by central Asian standards, and it was treating about 1,000 dismembered and disabled Afghan citizens a month, most maimed by some of the estimated 10 million land mines scattered throughout the country. The Canadian government had stipulated that their funds were dependent on women being treated and employed as well as men. Indeed, in the basement of this two-storey structure, eight women were treating disabled women who were hidden from the men upstairs.

Women Under the Taliban

It was there that I met secretly with a group of women to talk about their lives under the Taliban. They shed the burkas—

which make them look like clones of one another—and the contrast was shocking. Under those alienating veils were pretty, vibrant, engaging women. They were teachers before the Taliban closed the schools in Kandahar. Now they were sitting behind windows painted over so no one could see them. They weren't allowed to send their own daughters to school.

As women do, they made the visit unforgettable, with stories about their families, kibitzing about the job, and offers of cups of the traditional green tea and delicious, hot naan bread. I noticed they wore shoes with wedges and asked why they are all the same. At first they responded as if by rote and said, "High-heeled shoes are un-Islamic." I gestured to the painted windows and asked them how they put up with this nonsense. One woman blurted out, "It's unbearable." The others quickly hushed her. Then they looked at each other and the floodgates opened. "Look at this place, it's like a jail. Women are nothing in Afghanistan today. And our shoes, they're awful. We have to wear them because the Taliban don't like the tap-tap-tap of women's high-heeled shoes. We hate having to do this." They told me of a friend who went to jail for 30 days because she invited a foreigner to a family wedding, and another who was jailed for 15 days because she spoke to a man on the street. Every day was a struggle to buy enough food to feed their children. They were trying to keep their kids in the clandestine schools, but the classes were stopped so often that their education had become hit and miss, mostly miss.

"Look at this place, it's like a jail. Women are nothing in Afghanistan today."

During the time I spent listening to the extraordinary events of their lives, the women and I laughed and cried together. We made friends with each other. When I left, they tucked pieces of bread and sweet cakes into my pockets for the long journey out of their country. I knew I would never forget the sweet-faced Sharifa Reza Mohseny and the good-humoured, witty Frozan Mahram and her comical friend Sima Shahnawaz and the other women who worked with them. Nor would I forget their little children who were paying such a terrible price for the wreckage the merciless regime had inflicted on the country. It was truly humbling to receive from women who need so much to be given to them. They had the grace to worry about the comfort of someone else's voyage out of a country that had become their prison.

The street scene was the first sign of change.
Crowds of men and women walked on the street.

In the kind of Alice Through The Looking Glass contradiction that seems to be everywhere in Afghanistan, I learned that the Institute also provided prosthetics for those who had lost limbs in the grisly amputations mandated by the Taliban's interpretation of Sharia law. For stealing, the thief lost a hand, for stealing again, a foot. Therapist Zareen Khan was quick to point out, "The thief receives an injection of anaesthetic before the removal of the limb and so it is painless." Not so for women who were sentenced to death by stoning for alleged illicit relations. There was no numbing their pain. In fact, the Taliban's Sharia stated that the stones thrown not be so big as to kill them quickly.

An Afghan woman teaches an all-female class in March 2002. Since the fall of the Taliban, women can openly attend school.

When I bid farewell to the women I met during that voyage, their canny analysis and witty descriptions about their lives under the Taliban gave way to darker realities. With trepidation and in barely audible whispers, they implored me to take their story to the world outside, to ask the women in the world to help them. They said, "Get our schools open, get us back to work, or get us out of here."

After the U.S.-Led War

On Feb. 8 [2002], I returned to the country in the wake of the U.S. bombing campaign that overthrew the Taliban. I wanted to find out what was happening to women in Kabul and to try to find Sharifa and Frozan and the other women I'd met in Kandahar just one year earlier. The street scene was the first sign of change. Crowds of men and women walked on the street. While the vast majority of women still wore burkas, change was clearly happening from the bottom up. Forced to wear wedge-heeled shoes during the Taliban era, and forbidden to wear white socks or any other form of stocking that might attract attention, the women of Kabul were making a statement, feet-first. Platform shoes, high heels, patent-leather pumps were everywhere. And hosiery was patterned, coloured and very much on display. Even the burkas were at a jaunty angle, displaying dresses. Hands, formerly hidden, were very much in evidence while women walked together, talking, gesturing, and even returning the thumbs-up sign to me when we passed on the street. There was a palpable air of excitement in the city— and music, which had also been forbidden, was playing at every little kiosk. Women were working again and not wearing burkas in the offices. Girls' schools had re-opened, and the students were trying to catch up on what they had missed. And the girls were writing entrance exams to get back to university.

> *Life was looking very different from the ordeal they were living through when last we met.*

When I arrived in Kandahar, the shrieks and laughter of children at play filled the air, a sound I had never heard during the Taliban occupation, when children were forbidden to play, even with their own toys. We drove to the Institute of Orthopedics and, to my surprise, the first person to greet me was Zalmai Mojadidi, my former fixer. "Your girls are waiting for you," he said jubilantly. And suddenly there they were—Sharifa, Frozan, Sima, Torpeky, Zarghona and Rozia. The reunion was wonderful, exhilarating, and very emotional. Everyone talked at once, telling me where they'd been during the American bombing, how they felt when the Taliban were defeated. And each one in turn shared her hopes for tomorrow. "Now we have freedom," said Frozan Mahram. "Every girl can go to school. We can watch TV, walk in the street. If a woman wants to wear a burka or not, she can. We can choose our own husbands and they don't have to have beards."

Sima Shanawaz, who had been married just a month before we met in January, 2001, put her new baby boy, Tariq, into my arms and said, "See what I did." The paint had been scrubbed off the windows in their therapy department, and their wedge shoes replaced with fashionable pumps. Sharifa Reza Mohseny said her six children could now have an education. Her daughter Sima, 15, who hadn't been to school in five years, told me she wanted to be a doctor and take care of the sick people in Kandahar.

Life was looking very different from the ordeal they were living through when last we met. "The bazaar is full of video cassettes and music," said Sima. "People are singing and dancing. There are marriage ceremonies. We watch American films on television." The rapid-fire accounts of their lives then were told as though to annul the long years they lived in what seemed to be a prison. They told me they wanted to travel, to see foreign countries, to have peace and freedom. They wanted education, a modern lifestyle, streets and hospitals that functioned. They used to be afraid of everything, even the staff at this centre, even each other at times.

We had tea and talked about families and promised to stay in touch. They posed for a photo with me and said, "This time you can use our family names and our faces. We're safe now. We're not afraid anymore."

5

Warlords in Afghanistan Are Once Again Threatening Human Rights

John Sifton

The Taliban's human rights abuses were well documented before the U.S.-led attack in 2001. Immediately after the defeat of the Taliban, human rights in Afghanistan greatly improved. As time went on, though, heavily armed tribal warlords began to assert their dominance throughout Afghanistan and committed new atrocities. As Human Rights Watch researcher John Sifton explains in the following selection, reports of the abuse perpetrated by warlords are circulating throughout the country. Many families do not let their daughters attend school out of fear they will be kidnapped or raped by gunmen working for the government. Some women have been threatened with death for advocating women's rights. Those abuses may grow worse, Sifton says, and portend a terrible future for Afghanistan. To remedy this situation, according to Sifton, the United States must disarm and end its support of the warlords and help to develop an increased police presence throughout the country.

H uman Rights Watch believes that human rights conditions in Afghanistan—which of course had improved dramatically with the collapse of the Taliban—are now in a state of deterioration.

Our most recent research shows that, in many districts and villages in Afghanistan today, families are now living in a constant state of fear. Most of the country is in the hands of warlords and gunmen—fighters in Afghanistan's past wars—who are now terrorizing local populations under their authority, robbing houses at night, stealing valuables, killing people, raping young women and girls, raping boys, seizing land from farmers, extorting money, and kidnapping young men and holding them until their families can pay a ransom. The situation is of course different in each district, but in almost every district Human Rights Watch has visited in the last six months [2003], we have heard complaints about some or all of these types of abuses.

My colleagues have interviewed women who have been threatened with death for advocating women's rights.

I have interviewed numerous families myself who have been robbed in the night by Afghan military troops or police, and listened to witnesses describe being beaten by troops, and begging for mercy.

But sadly there is more: our research has also uncovered cases of Afghan military commanders and officials—including high-level Afghan government officials—threatening and arresting journalists and political organizers, and beating or even torturing perceived opponents. I have interviewed myself several people who were tortured by Afghan government security forces, for organizing dissident political parties or groups. My colleagues have interviewed women who have been threatened with death for advocating women's rights.

Consequences of Abuse of Power

Of course, these abuses are bad enough on their own, but their consequences for Afghanistan's future are even worse.

In many areas, Afghan civil society organizers, political organizers, and women's rights activists are now terrified of the warlord-rule, which makes it impossible for them to speak or organize openly. Many political organizers are now operating in secret. Journalists, in [the capital city of] Kabul and elsewhere, are censoring themselves. The situation, to put it mildly, does not bode well for Afghanistan's upcoming constitutional loya jirga [grand tribal assembly] or elections in 2004.

The continuing instability is also keeping many refugees in Iran and Pakistan from returning home. We talked to many returned refugees, who were stuck in Kabul city, unable to return to the more dangerous rural areas. "We wish we had stayed in Pakistan," some of them said.

The worst consequence by far, however, has been the effect of the insecurity on the lives of women and girls.

Afghan Women and Girls Live in Fear

Here in the United States, administration officials, and the President himself, have repeatedly said that Afghanistan has been liberated, and noted that girls have gone back to school.

The reality is more sobering. In many areas of Afghanistan today, insecurity is in fact forcing women and girls to stay indoors, and is depriving them of the opportunity to attend schools, go to work, or even seek health care at clinics and hospitals. We talked to countless families who affirmed this.

We are not talking about crime here, we're talking about human rights abuses by government forces.

[In 2003] the U.N. estimated that only thirty-two percent of school children in Afghanistan were girls. Population statistics in Afghanistan are always somewhat hit or miss, but under even the most conservative government estimates, it is clear that the majority of school-age girls in Afghanistan are not attending school. UNICEF estimates that in some provinces, the attendance rate for girls is as low as three percent.

Why are girls not in school? Some people think there is a "cultural" reason, having to do with entrenched Islamic conservatism. Our research does not support such a conclusion.

Instead, the reasons in many cases seem to be security-based. In many provinces, especially around Kabul, Afghan families tell us that they aren't letting their daughters go to school because they fear they will be assaulted by gunmen on the way, kidnapped or raped. Many say that they *want* to send their daughters to school, but cannot, because of insecurity.

At some time in the future, the situation in Afghanistan could very well explode.

Let me be clear about what we are talking about with all of these abuses: We are not talking about crime here, we're talking about human rights abuses by government forces: warlords and gunmen who ostensibly work for the Afghan government. We are talking about abuses by the leftover militias of the Northern Alliance and other anti-Taliban forces, the irregular military forces who work in some areas with the United States military, and the current police forces made up of former military personnel. These forces were the allies of the United States in its war against the Taliban regime, and were armed, assisted, and enabled by the U.S. government.

These words we use—"warlords" and "warlordism"— are not mine but those of Afghans themselves. They are Persian and Pashto words, translated into English: in Persian, the words *jang salar*, warlords; *tufangdar*, gunmen (*topakyan* in Pashto); *jang salari*, or *jang salarism*, warlordism, the rule of the gun. These are the words Afghans themselves are using to describe those who terrorize them.

And this is the vocabulary of Afghanistan today. This is the result of the Taliban's totalitarianism being replaced by the violence and cruelty of unfettered warlordism.

Cease International Funding of Warlords

You have heard from other witnesses today about the need for increased peacekeeping outside of Kabul, for more U.S. involvement in disarmament, demobilization, and reintegration of former fighters (including a better vetting procedure, to sideline those with abusive pasts), and the need for funding for policing forces. Human Rights Watch seconds all of these recommendations. We also think that the U.S. should insist that the United Nations increase its human rights monitoring efforts.

But we would add that there is also a need for the U.S., and all other nations involved in Afghanistan, to cut off support for the warlords themselves. We urge specifically the Department of Defense, the Defense Intelligence Agency, and the Central Intelligence Agency—all of whom are cooperating with local military leaders in Afghanistan—to take better steps to avoid strengthening local military leaders.

As it stands, the United States has a split strategy in Afghanistan—supporting [president] Hamid Karzai on the one hand, but cooperating with local warlords to hunt former Taliban on the other. Indeed, U.S. officials have for the most part just stood by and allowed local military leaders to seize control of local governmental offices—not only military bases, but health departments, trash collection offices, transportation ministry offices, and so on. This is not a good policy. Oftentimes, it seems that U.S. military and intelligence officials have assumed that, because Afghan forces are helping them, these forces are good and honorable people. This is an untenable view.

One last point: At some time in the future, the situation in Afghanistan could very well explode. When that happens, it is more than likely that most people in the world will not blame the United Nations, or the people of Afghanistan. They will, however, blame the United States—which has been involved in Afghanistan's internal affairs for almost a quarter century.

It is vitally important for the U.S. administration to take action now to avoid such an outcome, and we strongly urge all of the members of this committee to urge them to do so. The U.S. must give more support to President Karzai in his efforts to bring warlords under control, and make better efforts to cut off the warlords themselves.

I will end with the words of a displaced Afghan man from a rural area who told us he was unable to return to his home district because of the security problems there. He told me:

> The gunmen, who have guns in their hands, are irresponsible forces. The United States, in a way, brought them to power, and it is these gunmen who create problems now for our people. These people must be disarmed. This is the foremost, most important step to be taken, immediately. Guns must only be given to those who have been trained. You must raise our voice to the United States, to disarm these people.

I very much hope I have done so today.

6

U.S. Intervention Has Improved Conditions in Afghanistan

S. Frederick Starr

Despite the military, economic, and political challenges presented by a post-Taliban Afghanistan, the United States has made some significant advances in liberating and reconstructing the country. According to S. Frederick Starr, chairman of the Central Asia–Caucasus Institute, Afghanistan has clearly benefited from the U.S.-led attack on Afghanistan and the subsequent reconstruction efforts. In this selection he argues that Afghanistan is a much safer and potentially a more stable place thanks to the ousting of al Qaeda and its Taliban hosts and to the U.S.-led rebuilding of necessary Afghan governmental institutions and infrastructure. Although much remains to be accomplished in Afghanistan, he says, it is necessary to acknowledge the projects that have thus far been successful in order to ensure future progress.

It is no secret that the U.S. has its hands full in Afghanistan. Warlords masquerading as "regional leaders," criminal Islamists, heroin trafficking, and general lawlessness are but a few of the immediate challenges. And then there are the longer-term realities: severe poverty, a total lack of infrastructure, etc.

Faced with all this, pundits in Europe and America have been quick to declare a U.S. failure. They view Afghanistan

S. Frederick Starr, "A Sweet Sixteen: Plenty of Reasons to Cheer the Post-Taliban Afghanistan," *National Review*, vol. 55, August 11, 2003. Copyright © 2003 by National Review, Inc., 215 Lexington Ave., New York, NY 10016. Reproduced by permission.

as a kind of quicksand, where effort only gets one stuck deeper. Ultimately, they claim, America's resolve will flag and the whole mission will come undone.

Many elements of this diagnosis are on target: Monstrous problems rise up on every side in Afghanistan, and they are not getting simpler over time. But before we declare defeat and run from the scene, it would be well to weigh the challenges against what the U.S. has accomplished over the past year and a half. Seen in perspective, the situation in Afghanistan is far more positive than the doomsayers would imagine.

Successes in Afghanistan

For starters, the U.S. destroyed the Taliban government— and left al-Qaeda on the defensive by driving [it] into the frontier areas of Pakistan. There is still armed resistance to the Karzai government, but it now arises from local opportunists playing on local dissatisfactions, rather than from a coherent national—let alone international—force.

Second, vigorous measures by the U.S. averted the mass famine that was universally predicted in the dry autumn of 2001. The U.N. also played an important role in preventing this disaster, but nine-tenths of its funds for humanitarian relief came from America. The same goes for the many non-governmental organizations that provided significant help, most of which operated under contracts with U.S. government agencies. Since the American government does not require that the source of support be indicated, few Afghan beneficiaries (or, for that matter, Western reporters) are aware of this.

The situation in Afghanistan is far more positive than the doomsayers would imagine.

Third, moving with astonishing speed, the U.S. managed to distribute tons of hybrid seeds to even the most remote parts of Afghanistan, immediately multiplying yields across that parched land. Given that thousands of acres of agricultural land are still riddled with land mines, this initiative not only helped provide sustainable sources of food for millions but also saved thousands from death or maiming. As the people once more become able to feed themselves through agriculture, the lure of the warlords' meager stipends will fade and village economies will revive.

Fourth, while thousands of anti-tank and anti-personnel mines still litter the land, the U.S. has destroyed 10,000 mines in Kandahar province alone, and the pace of land-mine removal has quickened recently.

Fifth, firmness at key moments by the U.S. Army pre-vented the eruption of the massive regional war that was so widely predicted. In a country in which 2 to 3 million people have been slaughtered over a quarter century, this is no mean achievement.

Sixth, even though Afghanistan still has no national army, the U.S. has successfully trained nine battalions of the new professional forces. And while these units are still un-balanced numerically in favor of Tajiks from the north—a problem that the U.S. is working to address—they provide the core of a professional army which, over time, will re-place the warlord gangs that have controlled the field since the collapse of the old Afghan royal government [in the 1970s]. Moreover, the task of training will get easier as Afghans come to accept that a professional military is once more possible in their country.

The new Afghan government . . . successfully recalled all of the money in circulation and introduced a stable new currency.

Seventh, even though the U.S. does not provide troops for the International Security Assistance Force (the U.N.-sanctioned peacekeeping troops), it plays the key role in re-cruiting soldiers from many countries for that purpose, as well as in coordinating the force and providing logistical support and intelligence. The U.S. has also begun the largest program to date for police training. Germany and other countries have also contributed responsibly to this, but the U.S. commitment dwarfs the rest, as does the thor-oughness of the training it offers.

Eighth, the Afghan economy cannot recover until the major highways are reconstructed. The U.S. not only spear-headed the international effort to rebuild the crucial "ring road" linking Kabul, Herat, and Kandahar—and committed far more money to that effort than any other country—it is also far ahead of all others in the actual construction work.

Ninth, with close U.S. involvement and strong U.S. support, the new Afghan government and its talented finance minister, Ashraf Ghani, successfully recalled all of the money in circulation and introduced a stable new currency that has earned confidence nationally. All arrears with the IMF [International Monetary Fund] have been cleared as well. Given the number of well-established governments that have found these tasks impossible, this is no mean feat.

These developments are due directly to American leadership and support.

Tenth, the U.S. provides solid backing to official Afghan efforts to hack back the mafia economy that grew up after the fall of the Taliban. Thanks in good measure to U.S. support, Afghanistan now has a development plan that is both ambitious and responsible. The so-called Ghani Plan systematically removes impediments to the operation of healthy market forces, and promises to release the entrepreneurship and trading skills for which Afghans have been renowned over the centuries.

Eleventh, confounding doubters on every side, the U.S., again working closely with the Karzai government, ensured that schools were reopened as planned in the spring of 2002. Equally important, new textbooks were efficiently printed and distributed. True, a total of some 1,000 schools need to be rebuilt, but with several hundred already reopened, America is in a good position to engage other countries and donors in this crucial project.

Twelfth, thanks mainly to the security environment provided by the United States, the Loya Jirga, or National Assembly, was held in June 2002, with the result that its 1,500 delegates overwhelmingly backed the principle of a moderate form of government for Afghanistan. This was a crucial step in legitimizing the Karzai government for the period extending down to the 2004 elections.

Thirteenth, even though Afghanistan is far from being a democracy, the country still enjoys a greater degree of openness and freedom today than at any time in decades—despite constant intimidation by local warlords. Scores of newspapers and periodicals are available (some solid, others scurrilous), and both national radio and the embryo of rational television now exist.

Fourteenth, a small U.S. force assigned to protect President Karzai has enabled him to work in relative security, gradually strengthening the new government, even at a time when political assassinations continue to occur with alarming frequency.

Fifteenth, where formerly Afghanistan existed behind a Chinese wall of religious extremism and constant warfare, today its new national government has opened over 30 embassies abroad, the national airline is functioning again, legal trade has reopened with countries on every side, and thousands of legitimate businessmen enter and leave Afghanistan daily. This has not yet cut into the massive illegal drug trade or the widespread piracy, but over time it is bound to do so.

Sixteenth, buoyed by a new confidence engendered by the above developments, more than 2 million Afghan refugees have returned to their homes from squalid camps in Pakistan and Iran. None were compelled to do so, and all managed to find their own way back without external assistance. Besides representing a stunning vote of confidence in a peaceful future, this repatriation helps "drain the swamp" of festering discontent in the kind of refugee camps that gave rise to the Taliban in the first place.

Real Progress Has Been Made

Clearly, every one of these achievements must be qualified with "but," "although," or "in spite of." The entire effort is, as they say, a work in progress. But it is not an effort that is going nowhere, let alone one that is in reverse gear. On the contrary, these and other developments today will change Afghanistan's economic and political landscape, and eventually its psychological landscape as well.

In every case, these developments are due directly to American leadership and support. In some cases this leadership is exercised alone; in others it has involved collaboration with other countries or international agencies. In many instances the leadership comes from governmental agencies far removed from the Pentagon or State Department—whether Agriculture, Commerce, or the Treasury. In still others, it is channeled through competent non-governmental organizations in the United States and elsewhere.

It would be naive to understate the problems that exist in Afghanistan, and dangerous to minimize the gravity of the crisis that will boil up if they are not addressed. But to deal effectively with these issues requires, among other things, a sober appreciation of the many areas where progress is in fact occurring. Such an assessment can only underscore the overriding importance of solid planning, careful implementation, judicious collaboration, and sheer tenacity in the months and years ahead.

A hunger for catastrophe has suffused many recent commentaries on Afghanistan. But while a practical acknowledgement of achievements and shortcomings alike can help ensure more effective action in the future, crisis-mongering only breeds crises. The doomsayers are like farmers who, about this time of year, start pulling up corn to see how the roots are doing. And their dire predictions about what could go wrong in Afghanistan take little account of what we have done right.

Chapter 3

U.S. Involvement in Reconstructing Afghanistan

1

Without U.S. Support, the Afghan State Could Collapse

Ishaq Shahryar

In the aftermath of the U.S.-led attack on Afghanistan and the collapse of the Taliban government, an interim authority was established by the United Nations to govern Afghanistan. The purpose of this government was to begin reconstructing the war-torn nation and to restore law and order after decades of civil war. In this report to the U.S. Senate Foreign Relations Committee, Ishaq Shahryar, Afghan ambassador to the United States, describes a grateful and hopeful Afghanistan on the verge of sliding back into chaos and ruin. Shahryar makes it clear that although Afghanistan is making progress, its continued success is heavily dependent on massive U.S. and other foreign aid. While Afghanistan desires to be self-sufficient, Shahryar says, the fledgling nation needs continued U.S. economic and military support or it might witness a replay of the events that allowed the Taliban to seize power.

It is a great honor to be with you today and to share some thoughts about an important, perhaps even vital, work in progress in Afghanistan.

Given the heroic investment of American dollars and American lives in the liberation and rebuilding of Afghanistan it is most appropriate that you have a progress report direct from the beneficiary.

Ishaq Shahryar, address to the U.S. Senate Foreign Relations Committee, Washington, DC, February 12, 2003.

And that is what I will provide here today—with the overarching theme that America's investments in Afghanistan are commensurate with the returns, returns that can be measured in terms of eliminating the scourge of terrorism, enhanced regional and global security—and with enhanced security comes enhanced economic growth. . . .

I believe there can be redemption through suffering. And perhaps the greatest and most lasting redemption throughout this entire saga may come to pass for the women of the world. When the world began to see full force the systematic brutalization and discrimination against the women of Afghanistan by the Taliban gangsters,—I believe that leaders of the world and in this chamber resolved to mount a renewed effort to end all forms of discrimination against all women in all nations of the world. . . .

We are a country the size of Texas and we have a great deal to be thankful for. We are a grateful nation, thanking the world's most generous nation. My words of gratitude would still be insufficient if I spend my entire allotted time thanking the long list of Americans who have embraced Afghanistan—workers from our government agencies, NGO [nongovernmental organizations] and private companies.

But instead, I would prefer to turn to the actions and plans in place and going forward that will bring lasting and positive change to the region and best represent the gratitude of the Afghan people.

I am new to the diplomacy business. My residence and professional experience of the last 45 years has been centered in Southern California where I have been taking English lessons. So I trust there will be no need for translation.

I would like to begin my remarks with a simple observation and to present context for this hearing.

Instability in Afghanistan

The observation: The official name of my country, as indicated on our passports, is "The *Transitional* Islamic Republic of Afghanistan."

"Transition" is a key phrase and umbrella theme for my remarks this morning. We are a work in progress—and in a context.

And the context is this: Two decades ago a very bright professor named Brzezinski referred to our region in the Middle East, the north and west side of the great mountains that divide Asia from Europe, as the *Arch of Instability*.

But in recent years, without question, that arch has become a *Circle of Instability*—matched by an arch that extends across the southern and eastern side of the mountainous continental fence—and includes Pakistan, India, Bangladesh and even as far as Indonesia.

At the center of this circle is Afghanistan. Afghanistan is at the center of today's "Circle of Instability."

But this is not new. It is history repeating itself. For 4,000 years, Afghanistan has been a "portal" for history . . . more than just a crossroads . . . a portal.

For most of human history, travel from Europe or the Middle East to Asia could only pass one way—through Afghanistan, and through the Khyber Pass.

Genghis Khan, Tamerlane, Alexander the Great, to name a few, crossed Afghanistan and left their mark on Afghan government, arts and sciences.

Afghanistan is at the center of today's "Circle of Instability."

Others, of course, entered and occupied Afghanistan as well, but left behind only destruction and chaos. In our generation, it was the Soviets in the 1980s, and the Taliban of the 1990s.

I offer this brief history lesson to suggest the following: Afghanistan is literally the "high ground" of history.

Control the Afghanistan high ground, and you will influence for good or for evil that which flows into Europe and into Asia.

If the Western World has a lapse of attention and turns elsewhere, the "institutional memory" of the region will leach back in to a weak Afghanistan with drugs, corruption, and terror—and invariably "the circle" will turn back toward terror and conflict.

If the Western World sustains support and stays focused and present until democracy and prosperity are firmly rooted, then Afghanistan will become a hub, a hub of regional stability, democracy and prosperity that will become self-sustaining.

This is not theory—it is a replay of another recent and successful deployment of U.S. and international will on a smaller scale, where foresight was acted upon indeed, the foresight of this Committee was acted upon and conflict on a broad scale was essentially prevented.

I invite you to compare the regional geopolitical situation of land-locked, impoverished, but historically very significant Afghanistan in the Middle East and Asia to that of land-locked, impoverished, but very historically significant Macedonia in the Balkans.

As you know from history, Macedonia in many ways is the historic portal that connects Europe and the Middle East, in the same way that Afghanistan is the portal that connects Asia and the Middle East.

There, for the first time in history, the U.S. and NATO, very smartly, put a military presence in Macedonia before conflict spilled into that historic tinderbox.

Yes, there have been minor flashes of conflict in Macedonia, as flashes of conflict continue today in Afghanistan. But that historic "center of Balkan instability" was made secure and regional conflict was avoided—a conflict that might have brought two NATO powers to blows.

The analogy of that successful and modest investment holds for Afghanistan and the current Circle of Instability in the Middle East.

Poverty is the soil where terrorism takes root and makes the whole process of democracy, stability, and security impossible.

Consider the following comment from [Pakistani journalist] Ahmed Rashid, writing in the *Far Eastern Economic Review* in an article titled "A Desire to Be Left Alone"—with a tagline: Afghanistan's power-hungry neighbors threaten to revive the ruinous civil war of the early 1990s that gave rise to the Taliban.

> Russia is arming one warlord, Iran another. Wealthy Saudis have resumed funding Islamic extremists and some Central Asian Republics are backing their ethnic allies. India and Pakistan are playing out an intense rivalry as they secretly back opposing forces. The playing field is Afghanistan, and the interference threatens to revive a multifaceted power struggle that in the early

1990s eventually gave way to a near-ruinous rule by the Taliban.

This is pretty straight talk.

It doesn't get more concise in describing the cycle of the 1990s and what could re-emerge or can clearly be prevented if the U.S. and world community remain invested in the security and rebuilding of Afghanistan.

Perhaps it is a stretch to ever envision Afghanistan as a "Switzerland of the Middle East." But I find it useful to think in those terms.

We must begin with the premise that Afghanistan, like every other sovereign nation, is for the Afghan people and not the playing field for regional rivalries. And we must begin with this premise and hold firmly to it.

Afghanistan's History of Dictatorship

The institutional memory in the region reaches back 4,000 years. And regrettably that institutional memory favors dictatorship over democracy and economic suppression over economic prosperity.

And the bad habits that go with that history include devoting resources to developing nuclear, chemical, and biological weapons to enforce repression at the expense of economic opportunity and prosperity for people.

Look at Iran and Iraq, two countries blessed with immense petroleum wealth, where people live in poverty.

Repression is a medieval concept that does not belong in the 21st century.

- The denial of personal liberty removes transparency in government that leads to corruption.
- Corruption repels investment and economic development.
- Poverty is the soil where terrorism takes root and makes the whole process of democracy, stability, and security impossible.

Now, I know that I am preaching to the choir here.

These concepts are second nature to you. But there are novel, if not radical concepts to the hundreds of millions of people in the Middle East and South Asia.

I have heard some say that openness and democracy conflict with our Middle Eastern culture and tradition.

Nonsense.

It was Cyrus the Great of Persia who issued the world's first secular declaration of human rights.

Yes, there have been periods of greatness in the Middle East. But to date, the ancient cultures have failed to translate themselves into modern times, because there has been no one to lead beyond the past with the knowledge and convictions that—

- Theocracies fail;
- Dictatorships fail; but
- Democracy, somewhat more cumbersome to implement, works.
- But I believe, however, that the cycle of history in Afghanistan is being broken by leadership with a new vision.

Emerging Signs of Liberation

The people of Afghanistan have rallied to President Hamid Karzai as the one person who is truly able to unify Afghanistan, and turn the nation from a past filled with war and repression to a future focused on prosperity and democracy.

We began our future with liberation and with the restoration of our spirit. For a country that has literally been reduced to rubble, it is our creative spirit and our culture that anchors our new beginning.

To be frank, there is little else in our country that will hold an anchor.

With liberation, we've had the opportunity to reclaim our culture: our art, our music, our educational systems, our entrepreneurship—our freedom to create was given back to us. The grays and blacks imposed on us by the Taliban are being replaced by color.

- Our men can again play music.
- Our women and girls are returning to schools.
- And our children can again fly kites.

You've seen these things on CNN. You also know that we have a long way to go:

- 1 in 5 children born today will not reach the age of 5 years;
- 1 in 10 Afghan women will die in childbirth, leaving her other children as orphans;
- Of Afghanistan's 27 million people, the United Nations estimates nearly a quarter are refugees; and
- Afghanistan is the most heavily mined country in the

world. And as is the case in other war zones, children at play will become the victims of left-over land mines.

Addressing the humanitarian issues, the security issues, the rebuilding issues, and the economic development issues is not simple.

It has meant an international collaborative effort and to date, this multi-national collaboration is working—and working better than perhaps any comparable effort since the Marshall Plan.

Rebuilding—Cultural and Tangible

We have a rare and historic opportunity in Afghanistan—to change the course of a region that has triggered substantial global turmoil for the last generation, and been the focus of U.S. foreign policy for the last 18 months, and I dare say will be for the next 18 months.

With respect to rebuilding and security concerns I would like to briefly describe:
- Where we have been;
- The works in progress being crafted with the tools at our disposal focusing on security and reconstruction;
- Where we can go—according to a rather urgent time-line.

In many ways Afghanistan still lingers in a honeymoon period where we are designing and building a new nation from a clean sheet of paper.

In the immediate post-Taliban defeat in Afghanistan, there were no universities, no army, no police, no TV, no newspaper, no banking system, no judiciary, very little food and even less way of health care. The only thing in abundance: Guns and land mines.

Looking back 12 months [since 2002], we established a triage plan to urgently fill institutional vacuums. It began with the Bonn Agreement that provided the political road map and an interim administration to make a start. We then quickly moved to right the most egregious wrongs of the Taliban.
- All women workers and students were immediately restored to their pre-Taliban positions. Today, women constitute over 50% of civil servants and teachers.
- Some three million children have gone back to school.
- His Majesty King Zahir Shah returned to Afghanistan after almost three decades.

- The Grand Decision Making Assembly known as the Loya Jirga was convened and 1,501 representatives from all over Afghanistan participated. And a woman was a candidate for Presidency.
- Over two million refugees from outside and internally displaced have gone back to their homes and villages.
- Liberal investment laws were passed to attract foreign and Afghan investors and free enterprise has re-gained a foothold.
- All state enterprises have become subject to open bidding.
- A neighborly conference was held in Kabul on the anniversary of Bonn Conference to mark our neighbors' commitment to non-interference, good neighborliness and mutual respect. This has resulted in the Kabul Declaration.
- National Defense Council, National Security Council, Civil Affairs Commission, Human Rights Commission, Constitutional Commission and many other entities have been established to speed up the work of the government.
- A Constitutional Commission was established, drafting began, and is now nearly completed. By the end of the year it will be completed and ratified by another Loya Jirga.
- And just like here in the United States, in 2004, we will again hold free and fair general elections.

Those were tangible acts of immediate need. There have also been needs to lay foundations for Cultural Reconstruction—the re-establishment of a national sense of identity and providing an education to the Afghan people—both of which are critical to ending factionalism of the sort that plagued Afghanistan in the aftermath of the Soviet defeat and withdrawal.

For years, the moral compass of the nation has been spinning like a top.

You see, for over 20 years the Afghan people have endured two attempts at brain-washing. First by the brutal far-left extremes of communism. Then by the brutal far-right extremes of the Taliban's "Thug Theocracy."

Is it any wonder the brains of our young people are scrambled?

For years, the moral compass of the nation has been spinning like a top.

We need to remind the adults of Afghanistan who they are, where they have been.

And at the same time we are telling our children that their entire lives, all that they have known for 20 years, is an aberration. That in the 21st century, open societies, freedom of thought, freedom of speech, freedom of commerce, freedom from want, fear and intimidation are the models for civil society and where the world is going.

To that end:

- We will hold fast to secular government.
- Work urgently to restore our libraries, our museums, our cultural monuments, and our national parks.
- We must also encourage the direction where the invisible hand of freedom has already led us—the creation of free and independent media. Indeed, there are already 150 new news organizations in Kabul and Kabul Radio is now up 24/7 and broadcasting to a national audience.
- We are working hard to create a judiciary system that is transparent, based on the rule of law and representative of the entire nation. To that end our new Judiciary Commission and Commission on Human Rights have been hard at work, and I am pleased to say that 200 women judges have been restored to the bench.

I think we have made great progress. Here is the testimony of Robert Oakley, former U.S. Ambassador to Pakistan, in a recent op-ed from the *Washington Post:*

Starting from zero a year ago, the administration of President Hamid Karzai has achieved many attributes of a responsible government.

- It has a long-term national development framework and budget, worked out with the World Bank, the United Nations, the United States and other donors, and is carefully applying it to ensure that donor proposals meet Afghan realities.

- A central bank, fiscal discipline and a new national currency have been established.

• Construction of the large-scale Ring Road program has begun; large-scale community development projects will soon follow smaller efforts.

• An Afghan Defense Commission (including senior "warlords") has reached agreement on the size, make-up and training of the new army and the demobilization of local militias.

Ambassador Oakley goes on to say what I firmly believe: "The key to this trend line continuing in a positive direction is the continued presence and focused attention of the United States of America."

America's Role in Reconstruction

The American effort has already been heroic, creative, and generous.

Consider, just in recent months:
• the Congress and Administration produced the $3.3 billion Afghan Freedom Support Act;
• Secretary [Colin] Powell unveiled the Administration's U.S.-Middle East Partnership Plan; and
• the President dispatched a special delegation of American women to Kabul under the auspices of U.S.-Afghan Women's Council.

But this trend line of attention and active support must continue into 2003. If it does, and I believe it will, the good news will continue and Afghanistan will become the first example in this new century and centuries to come—of what democracy can do for a struggling nation.

Last year [2002] began with $5 billion being pledged for the reconstruction of Afghanistan, including $1.8 billion for 2002, at the January 2002 Donor Conference in Tokyo. An additional $1.2 billion has been pledged for 2003. Although many major reconstruction projects had begun towards the end of the year, the majority of our population is living in poverty, below the pre-war 1976 levels in many cases.

The Loya Jirga that was held [in June 2002] helped to spur activity on a number of projects, including small scale initial recovery efforts, macro-reconstruction projects such as roads, energy and power, many of which were supported by funds channeled through UN agencies.

But, as Nigel Fisher, the UN Secretary General's Deputy Special Representative for Reconstruction, noted:

Tokyo pledges have largely been met, but the fundamental problem is that those pledges fall far short of the level of international assistance required to really kick-start Afghanistan's recovery. In per capita terms, the assistance provided to Afghanistan falls far short of aid provided for recovery from other major crises—in the Balkans, East Timor or Rwanda.

What's more, for the pledges that have not been met, checks are still in the mail, grants have been converted to loans, and many loans have become conditional or placed on hold.

The softening of global commitments to rebuild Afghanistan makes the U.S. commitment—as declared in last fall's Afghanistan Freedom Support Act—all the more important.

Our needs, living at the center of the "Circle of Instability" remain most urgent and we require significant financial support.

Our needs, living at the center of the "Circle of Instability" remain most urgent and we require significant financial support.

The landmark Afghanistan Freedom Support Act [which authorizes economic and military assistance to Afghanistan through 2005] that originated in this Committee provides a strategic framework for U.S. policy on the political and economic development of Afghanistan to provide that support.

- It protects and enhances the security of Afghanistan by authorizing military and security assistance, and supports counter-narcotics, crime control and police training activities for our government.
- The legislation also authorizes $1.7 billion in economic, humanitarian and development assistance in Afghanistan.
- Through the efforts of members of this distinguished panel, $300 million was provided for an Enterprise Fund to promote job creation and private sector development, and another
- $300 million in draw-down authority for military and other security assistance is authorized.
- The bill also provides a total of $1 billion to support

ISAF [International Security Assistance Force], if the President makes the necessary determinations.

We respectfully urge the Congress in this appropriations cycle to fully fund the Afghanistan Freedom Support Act.

The best way to secure our victory in Afghanistan is to secure democracy and build prosperity.

The Act created a template for reconstruction funding at not less than $450 million in fiscal year 2003. The need is urgent. Yet, the FY [fiscal year] 2003 Omnibus Budget looks like it will fall considerably short of the mark. I would urge you and your colleagues to bring the actual funding level up to the authorization mark so that funds can be deployed— not next year, but in the months ahead—to enhance education, improve health, especially for children, to strengthen our democratic institutions and to empower the women of Afghanistan.

As you are aware, President Bush will meet President Karzai in Washington toward the end of the month [February 2003] for talks on postwar reconstruction. President Bush has indicated that he looks forward to discussing with President Karzai "the progress being made toward our shared goals of rebuilding the country's society and economy, and securing a nation free from terror, war and want." We certainly are aware that President Bush has a great deal on his plate at this time. Thus, we are particularly grateful to him, to Secretary of State Powell and others in the Administration for their continued attention to Afghanistan and their commitment, in Secretary Powell's words, "to create an Afghanistan where terrorists and traffickers can never again flourish."

Keeping the Peace

And that leads me back to security—and the critical role of ISAF and its expansion to all corners of Afghanistan.

As you know, the transition to Dutch and German oversight of ISAF has gone smoothly. And going forward, we believe that this force, as it expands its mission beyond Kabul, will guarantee the long-term security of our entire country and make it possible for reconstruction efforts to succeed without terror or intimidation. Eventually—and I hope it will be sooner rather than later—we will establish, with the help of our allies, an effective military and police force to allow us to control our own destiny and our own affairs.

I urge this Committee to continue to support the expansion of ISAF, and I hope the Administration will make every effort to press America's friends and allies to join in this effort. . . .

Afghanistan internal security remains fragile. Recent outbursts of fighting, including air strikes yesterday against residual presence of Taliban and al Qaeda forces, remind us of the specter of oppression and terrorism that was only too real 18 months ago.

Non-interference from our regional neighbors is key. And the expansion of ISAF and the establishment of a national army will:

- demonstrate international support for the central government
- weaken the influence of regional leaders and their personal armies
- speed reconstruction and economic recovery
- increase the confidence of private investors
- promote stability and our ability to form a national army

The Afghan Army needs to be trained at a faster pace and bigger size. Two thousand men in one year are just not enough. Experts say that at least 700,000 guns are unaccounted for and it takes a strong army not only to collect them but also to counter the warlords. And their rapid deployment along with U.S. forces would not only make them better soldiers but also amount to a smaller number of casualties of U.S. armed services.

The expansion of ISAF is very good for all of the Afghan people—who have known only war for the last generation.

The expansion of ISAF will also help finish the job of extinguishing all vestiges of the Taliban and al Qaeda in Afghanistan so democracy has a chance—good for the Afghan people and the global community.

To that end, it is critical even in these times of global economic slow-down—that Afghanistan receive the promised security and financial assistance to help Afghanistan to recover, and rebuild.

Clearly, all nations stand to benefit from all new elements of stability in the Middle East, from any source.

Yes, Saddam Hussein is a very serious problem.

I am heartened that America and the world community are determined to deal with that despot.

And I pledge to you that Afghanistan will support whatever direction the U.S. and Allied nations take in dealing with Saddam Hussein—and winning another victory for democracy.

But let us also secure the victories that we have already won.

Challenges for the New Afghan Government

And the best way to secure our victory in Afghanistan is to secure democracy and build prosperity. And, the task of doing that centers squarely on the shoulders of the new government in Kabul and the international business community. And to no surprise, there is much to do.

- We need reliable electric power.
- We need to re-fill the hundreds of empty factories in our cities with workers—making textiles, cement, and other finished goods.
- We need to make a major commitment toward "big infrastructure development," like rebuilding our roads, that will bring jobs, and add to a national psychology of peace and security.
- Because 85% of the Afghan people are farmers, we need to embark on a massive program to support new agricultural initiatives—dams, irrigation canals and systems—that would employ millions of Afghans. This, combined with an alternate crop substitution for poppy farmers, could curtail illicit drug production tremendously.
- There needs to be a gradual shift from short-term humanitarian help to long-term sustainable development projects.
- Capacity building for the central authority means attracting the Afghan Diaspora, particularly, from the U.S. I appeal to you to consider additional funding for their provisional return back home to utilize their professional skills.
- Money is needed to fight the campaign against narcotics production, processing and trafficking, including its nexus to narco-mafia and cross-border instability.

- And we need to keep focused on Afghan's women and the establishment of centers for mothers and children in need—in need of literacy, vocational training, and especially medical care.

In closing, I hope I have offered useful assessment of where we are and where we hope to go.

I must be candid—we are not there yet, by any means. And if the progress that we have made in the past year or so is to continue, we will need help—financial help, technical assistance, and a certain amount of patience.

But I will say again, [this help] should not be viewed as altruism by the U.S. or world community. The returns to the U.S. and global security will be commensurate with the investment.

And I will also tell you that President Karzai and I are passionately determined not to squander this moment in Afghanistan's 4,000-year history.

Afghanistan has had enough political revolutions.

Afghanistan has been invaded and occupied by the armies of soldiers.

What we need today is to be occupied by a new benevolent kind of army: an army of teachers, doctors, builders, farmers, civil engineers, merchants, bankers and public safety experts—and perhaps even a few lawyers.

Note . . . I said "perhaps" to the lawyers . . . (as I mentioned . . . we have a special need to help clear mine fields . . .).

The goal here is a jump-start. Not a permanent occupying force. And many of you here in this room are in many ways part of this benevolent army.

We all need to make sure that the work undertaken on behalf of rebuilding Afghanistan is done in a manner which empowers the people of Afghanistan to take matters into their own hands.

As the Afghan proverb says, "A river is made drop by drop." Any great project, any important human undertaking, takes time and requires a long-term commitment. Clearly, the rebuilding of Afghanistan after more than 20 years of war and foreign occupation will take sustained effort and patience. And the timing is urgent.

Afghans are also a remarkably resilient people and a proud people—proud to learn, proud to do a good job.

As [British prime minister Winston] Churchill wisely stated, "Give us the tools and we will get the job done."

2

The United States Should Not Be Involved in Nation Building in Afghanistan

Subodh Atal

Two years after the U.S.-led war to rid Afghanistan of terrorists, leaders in many countries, including the United States, are calling for the United States to intensify its involvement in Afghanistan. They argue that the United States must play a pivotal role in helping Afghanistan build its political, economic, and military infrastructure, a process referred to as nation building. Independent foreign affairs analyst Subodh Atal contends, however, that any attempt at nation building in Afghanistan will fail as long as the security situation there remains unstable. Atal argues that many warlord power disputes and growing anti-U.S. sentiment in Afghanistan continue to destabilize the country's security situation. Moreover, he says, Afghanistan's traditional tribal and ethnic rivalries, a historical lack of a strong central government, and general distrust of foreign interference make Afghanistan a very poor candidate for nation building. Atal says that the United States should instead focus on destroying remnants of the Taliban and al Qaeda in order to bring peace to the region and create an atmosphere conducive to possible reconstruction.

Subodh Atal, "At a Crossroads in Afghanistan," *Foreign Policy Briefing*, September 24, 2003. Copyright © 2003 by the Cato Institute. All rights reserved. Reproduced by permission.

Two years after the events of September 11, 2001, and the subsequent defeat of the Taliban and al Qaeda by U.S.-led forces, Afghanistan remains highly unstable, and the U.S.-led war to rid the nation of Islamic extremists is faltering. According to numerous recent reports, the Taliban is regrouping, in partnership with al Qaeda remnants. Meanwhile, Gulbuddin Hekmatyar, a former Afghan prime minister and leader of the radical Islamic party Hizb-e-Islami, has called for a jihad against foreign occupiers and the creation of an Islamic state. The groups are attacking Afghan government targets, U.S. and other coalition forces, and civilian reconstruction projects. Warlords continue to feud with each other, undermining Afghan president Hamid Karzai's regime, and they have resuscitated the narcotics trade. Karzai is secure only inside his own compound, and doesn't trust his own defense ministry troops to act as his bodyguards.

In this worsening environment, there are renewed calls for the United States to intensify its involvement in Afghanistan. A report by the Council on Foreign Relations and the Asian Society recommends an expanded U.S. peacekeeping role, billions of dollars in new reconstruction aid, and active support for Karzai in his disputes with Afghan warlords. The Bush administration revealed in late July 2003 that it would request an additional $1 billion in aid for Afghanistan.

Policymakers should refuse to widen the U.S. role in Afghanistan's reconstruction.

Proponents of an increased U.S. commitment suggest that failed nations are potential hotspots for terrorist activity. In November 2001, Clare Short, then the British government's International Development Secretary, accused the United States of "turning its back" on the developing world, and she asserted that the alleviation of poverty worldwide was central to a global effort to fight terrorism. The United States has been admonished for "abandoning" Afghanistan after the Cold War, precipitating its descent into the Taliban-dominated era, and is now being criticized for not committing whole-heartedly to the nation's reconstruction following the war that ousted the Taliban. A report by Human Rights Watch chastised the U.S. government and other coalition partners for failing to restore order and security in the country, and called on the international community to rein in local and regional warlords and to expand peacekeeping operations. . . .

The security situation in Afghanistan is the biggest hurdle to such efforts. The nation is divided along ethnic lines, and feuding warlords further undermine the chances for sustaining a strong central government. The U.S. presence has already begun to trigger resentment and has even renewed sympathy for the Taliban in significant sections of the country. The Afghan situation closely parallels that of other countries where U.S. intervention failed in the past. Given America's prior experiences in similar situations, policymakers should refuse to widen the U.S. role in Afghanistan's reconstruction and focus instead on rapidly eliminating the anti-American forces that are resurgent in the region.

Calling for Nation Building in Afghanistan

President Karzai's visit to Washington in February 2003 was aimed at refocusing American attention back on his nation despite the impending war on Iraq and the other crises occupying center stage at the White House. While speaking to the Senate Foreign Relations Committee, Karzai reported a long list of achievements including the return of refugees and increased control by his central government over Afghan provinces, and he requested increased U.S. involvement and funds in various Afghan reconstruction efforts. Several individuals representing a diverse spectrum of opinion, including Sens. Chuck Hagel (R-Neb.), Barbara Boxer (D-Calif.), and Joseph Biden (D-Del.), responded favorably to Karzai's call for increased U.S. aid.

Less than a month later, the United Nations Security Council outlined a series of high-level political goals for Afghanistan, including the creation of "a multi-ethnic, gender-sensitive and fully representative government," with elections targeted for June 2004. Apart from the building of political institutions, other major Security Council goals that remain unfulfilled are enhancing internal security; disarming militias; countering the narcotics trade; building an effective, independent judiciary system; expanding human rights; improving health and education; and building critical infrastructure such as roads.

The costs of this ambitious set of goals are substantial. Michael O'Hanlon of the Brookings Institution estimates that between $15 billion and $50 billion is needed for the building of Afghanistan over a 10-year period and suggests that the United States provide at least 15 percent of the total aid to retain influence over "how the aid effort is administered and how the country is rebuilt."

One of the first prerequisites for successful nation building is a stable security situation.

"Assuming for the sake of argument," O'Hanlon continues, "a total annual aid package of $3 billion, the U.S. share might then be $400 million to $500 million." Over a 10- or 15-year period, such aid could total as much as $7.5 billion. As daunting as that figure seems (O'Hanlon offered his proposal in December 2001), the actual amount being spent in Afghanistan might already be much more. A report in the *New York Times* quoted unnamed American officials who projected that the cost in 2003 for operations in Afghanistan would likely equal the $935 million spent in the previous year. That figure did not include the cost of maintaining troops in the country and reflected expenditures on a number of civilian reconstruction projects including the building of roads and schools.

Other reports show American aid totaling more than $300 million, but it is not clear that this aid will be sustained at those levels for many years. The *Washington Post* reports that the $1 billion package proposed by the Bush administration in July 2003 is "designed to fund projects that can be completed within a year to have a maximum impact on the lives of the Afghan people" in order to boost the Karzai government prior to elections planned for October 2004.

Security Before Reconstruction

Notwithstanding past failures, many observers hold out hope that an American-led nation-building effort in Afghanistan will succeed. Such optimism ignores the fact that one of the first prerequisites for successful nation building is a stable security situation—the very condition that does not exist in Afghanistan. In the absence of a secure environment, nation-building efforts can get bogged down and eventually grind to a halt. [The Middle Eastern country of] Lebanon and Somalia [in Africa] are examples of situations in which external aid efforts were stymied by unresolved conflict and a lack of security. Combatants opposed to foreign intervention find it easy to sabotage reconstruction efforts, preventing civilian authorities and outside agencies from performing their tasks.

That is precisely what is happening in Afghanistan. In the words of Ramtanu Maitra of the *Asia Times*, "Afghanistan is not just dicey, but outright dangerous," and the situation there is hardly conducive to reconstruction. In this environment an Afghan vice president was assassinated [in 2002], and Karzai himself survived an attempt on his life in September 2002. In late January [2003], hundreds of U.S. soldiers, backed by air power, attacked radical Islamic militants in the Spin Boldak area in the Kandahar district. Soon thereafter, a powerful bomb blew up a civilian bus, killing 18 in Kandahar. By April, the militants had regrouped and were carrying out new attacks on U.S. and Afghan government targets. Aid workers were also targeted. Suspected Taliban loyalists killed two U.S. soldiers in March 2003 in an ambush, and two other U.S. military personnel died in a firefight in April. In July 2003, a landmine planted by the Taliban killed eight Afghan soldiers.

The Afghan rebels have demonstrated an ability to regroup and return after U.S. operations temporarily drive them out of their strongholds. This is especially true in the eastern provinces. It suggests that the militants have support in the tribal areas bordering Pakistan, where Pashtuns dominate. If a substantial part of Afghanistan remains under the grip of insurgents, the commitment of external resources—no matter how large—will be ineffective.

Warlord Games

Provincial and local leaders, better known as warlords, each backed by his own militia, have been the powerbrokers in Afghanistan since the days of the anti-Soviet resistance. The U.S. strategy of stabilizing Afghanistan following the collapse of the Taliban includes partnering with many of the warlords and securing their support for Karzai's central government. The warlords' agendas, however, do not parallel with those of the Americans. Many of the warlords have survived for decades through a combination of aid from external forces, their own ruthlessness, and a lucrative role in drug smuggling. The loyalties of these warlords are accordingly fickle, and they have little interest in supporting a strong central government that would encroach on their power.

Among the warlords who collaborated with U.S. forces to oust the Taliban is Abdul Rashid Dostum [former leader of the Northern Alliance] who controls the Uzbek-dominated territory around Mazar-e-Sharif. Dostum is funded by Uzbekistan, and may also be in the pay of Iran. Dostum's militia has clashed for control of northern Afghanistan with the forces of fellow Uzbek Mohammed Atta, and with those of Tajik leaders Burnahuddin Rabbani and Mohammed Fahim. Those sporadic battles prompted the UN to suspend aid operations in July 2002. Rabbani, a former prime minister, has his own ambitions of coming back to power in Kabul and is reportedly trying to influence local commanders by bribing them.

The loyalties of these warlords are . . . fickle, and they have little interest in supporting a strong central government that would encroach on their power.

In Herat, near the Iranian border, governor Ismail Khan has largely supported the United States but is reported to have connections to Iran, and has expressed impatience with the continued U.S. troop presence in the province. Khan's militia has clashed with that of a rival warlord, Amanullah Khan, who is reportedly supported by the Taliban. In this region, therefore, the United States faces an interesting dilemma, as it may be forced to choose between an Iranian-backed warlord and one connected to the Taliban.

Khan is challenged to the east by Gul Agha Sherzai. Sherzai's sphere of influence includes the provinces of Kandahar, Oruzgan, and Helmand, where the Taliban were strongest. Although Sherzai was "bought off" by millions of dollars in U.S. and British money, the amount was apparently not sufficient to deter him from clashing with rivals such as Khan.

In eastern Afghanistan, where infiltration across the Afghan-Pakistan border is a major concern, U.S.-led stabilization efforts also face considerable obstacles. Bacha Khan Zadran, whose militia operates in Khost and Paktia provinces, collaborated initially with U.S. Special Forces in the U.S.-led Operation Anaconda to drive out massing al Qaeda fighters in March 2002. In return for his support, Zadran was paid nearly a half a million dollars. Having secured that amount, Zadran assaulted the Khost capital of Gardez, home to a U.S. base. The May 2002 rocket attack killed more than 30 civilians. Last fall [2002], when U.S. forces asked Zadran to dismantle some checkpoints, rival leader Hakim Taniwal's fighters took it as a cue to attack Zadran's militia. Zadran, whose ambition is to rule over not only Khost and Paktia provinces, but also neighboring Paktika, has now turned against the United States. In March 2003, his militia attacked U.S. and Afghan government forces. In one of the clashes, Zadran's eldest son was killed, an incident that has only further alienated the warlord against the United States and the Afghan central government.

It is thus becoming increasingly clear that partnering with and bribing Afghan warlords is unlikely to accelerate the nation's recovery. The Soviets tried, and failed, to secure their hold on the country by buying the warlords' loyalty. The United States is experiencing a similar phenomenon.

Growing Anti-U.S. Resentment in Afghanistan

Insecurity and infighting among warlords are not the only impediments to a successful nation-building effort in Afghanistan. One of the many perils of nation building is that, despite the best intentions and efforts of the foreign power, the local population starts to resent its presence. This phenomenon was evident in Iraq as early as April 2003, mere days after the fall of Baghdad. After Saddam Hussein's ouster, many Iraqis—including Shias who had been suppressed by Hussein and who had been protected under the southern no-fly zone by the U.S.—turned against American troops. The anti-American feelings surprised the troops as well as America's wartime leaders. Americans are also surprised to learn that there is considerable resentment toward U.S. troops in South Korea, Japan, and Germany, where U.S. soldiers have been stationed for decades.

Many factors can contribute to such resentment, and each nation-building endeavor must contend with unique

circumstances. Afghans have bitter memories of Soviet occupation and have traditionally resisted the imposition of
foreign ideologies. In the past, once this resentment built
above a certain threshold, the presence of the foreign power
became a flashpoint for violent resistance, as happened to
the Soviets after the first year of their military intervention.
Going even further back in history, the first British invasion
[of Afghanistan] in 1838 was at first welcomed by some
Afghans. However, resentment against the foreign occupation built quickly, especially over the clash of cultures between the occupation forces and local Afghans. Shah Shuja,
the Afghan leader anointed by the British, was secure only
under their protection, similar to Karzai's situation today.

In the case of the U.S. presence in Afghanistan, several
mitigating factors have slowed the development of massive
resistance. Many Afghans opposed the Taliban and they
fought side by side with American troops to expel the medieval regime. Those individuals continue to work closely
with U.S. authorities. Other Afghans have simply tired of
the incessant fighting, and they look hopefully for a chance
for peace.

An initial welcome for foreign intervention can quickly
turn into a deeply antagonistic relationship, however. In
such situations, the presence of outside peacekeepers can
become counterproductive. In Afghanistan, there are signs
that resentment of the U.S. presence is building. Continued
conflict, including U.S. operations against Al Qaeda, have
killed and injured dozens of civilians. Notwithstanding the
unfortunate accidents that have claimed civilian lives, the
continued U.S. military presence also bruises cultural sensi-
tivities. Afghan civilians have complained of raids on their
houses by U.S. troops while women were present. Errant
U.S. bombs in civilian areas, including one that killed 11
civilians in April 2003, have exacerbated an already tense situation. On May 6, 2003, the first large-scale anti-U.S. pro-
test took place in Kabul.

Central Authority vs. Federal Structure

The bitter fighting among the various warlords and persistent foreign meddling have contributed to an ethnic fragmentation that cannot be readily overcome by nation-
building activities. Ethnic tensions were clearly exacerbated
during the period of anti-Soviet resistance [1979–1988]

when different factions were the beneficiaries of external assistance. However, the actual roots of those tensions are deeper. The British imperialists had a tough time keeping the region under their control and out of the Russian realm. The Afghan-Pakistan border is actually an artifact of British colonial rule. In the face of frequent and nagging Afghan resistance, the British drew an arbitrary line—the Durand Line—which demarcated Afghanistan from imperial India, and divided the rebellious Pashtuns. Populations on either side have never accepted the division, and today the Pashtun tribes on the Afghan side have more in common with their brethren across the Durand Line than they do with the Uzbeks and Tajiks in northern Afghanistan.

Each nation-building endeavor must contend with unique circumstances.

Those persistent ethnic tensions are equally important today, as Afghans and outsiders attempt to shape the nation's future. The southern Pashtuns harbor significant resentment over the degree of control that the Tajiks, Uzbeks, and Hazaras of the Northern Alliance have over the Karzai regime. While considerable attention is being paid to the establishment of a strong central government as a milestone of Afghanistan's nation-building process, the lack of respect commanded by Karzai's central government and the de facto autonomy practiced in the warlord-led Afghan provinces suggests that other alternatives to nation building should be considered. Above all, policymakers should recognize that it is unwise for external actors, including the United States, to dictate the structure of the Afghan government. A centralized regime imposed from the outside will likely result in further resentment against the United States. Given the deep divisions within the country, a federal structure, with a considerable degree of autonomy granted to provincial leaders, may be the only practical solution—but that decision should be left up to the people of Afghanistan.

Afghanistan's Entanglement in the Great Game

During the better part of the past two centuries, Britain and Russia competed for influence directly or indirectly in Afghanistan, which is strategically located at the crossroads between the Middle East, Central Asia, and the Indian sub-continent. After the British Empire crumbled [in the early twentieth century], the nation became a Cold War hotspot, with the Soviets steadily gaining the upper hand in the region. Paradoxically, the Soviets' influence waned after their invasion of the country in late 1979. After the Soviet military withdrawal, which began in 1988, and the collapse of the Soviet-backed Afghan government in 1991, Afghanistan gradually became an extension of the India-Pakistan conflict, with India supporting the Northern Alliance against the Pakistan-backed Taliban. The Northern Alliance was also supported by governments in Iran, Russia, Uzbekistan, and Tajikistan, which were all concerned about Taliban advances into their respective spheres of influence.

It is unwise for external actors, including the United States, to dictate the structure of the Afghan government.

The ousting of the Taliban regime has not altered the tendency of neighboring states to meddle in Afghan affairs. Russia, Uzbekistan, and Tajikistan still back various factors of the Northern Alliance, as does India, which has established consulates in Afghan cities close to the Pakistan border. Meanwhile, elements in the Pakistani intelligence service have helped the Taliban reconnect with the al Qaeda and with the resurgent forces of Gulbuddin Hekmatyar's Hizb-i-Islami. The United States supported the radical Islamic party during the years of Soviet occupation, but Hekmatyar and his followers have turned against their former patron, who they now see as yet another foreign occupier. In December 2002, Hekmatyar, a former Afghan prime minister, issued a statement declaring that Hezb-i-Islami would "fight our jihad until foreign troops are gone from Afghanistan and the Afghans have set up an Islamic government."

If the United States becomes more involved in Afghan civilian affairs, American interests will inevitably clash with those of one or more of the regional players vying for proxy influence in the country. Such entanglements are likely to further undermine Afghan security. Rather than keep forces in Afghanistan for the long term, the United States should accelerate operations aimed at eliminating the anti-U.S. forces now massing along the Afghan-Pakistan border but should otherwise avoid getting mired in a renewal of the so-called Great Game.

Preemptive Nation Building as a Policy Framework?

To assess the future of American policy in nations such as Afghanistan and Iraq, U.S. officials would do well to look at history and consider the results of past interventions. A recent study by the Carnegie Endowment for International Peace estimated that out of more than 200 military interventions by the United States since 1900, only 16 were aimed at creating democratic institutions. Of those 16, only 2 countries—Japan and Germany—made the successful transition to stable democratic governments. Two other nations—Grenada and Panama—are too small to be significant. In all other cases, there was no functioning democracy in place 10 years after the end of American involvement. It is impossible to predict whether there will be democracy in Afghanistan in [2013]; however, given the myriad aggravating factors in that country, including continued conflict, resistance to external meddling, and a cultural gap between western objectives and the traditional Afghan approach to problems, the prospects for successful nation building are bleak.

American interests will inevitably clash with those of one or more of the regional players vying for proxy influence in the country.

Nonetheless, there has been no shortage of calls for nation building. Much of this derives from the argument that terrorism thrives amidst poverty and political chaos. Susan Rice of the Brookings Institute classifies a large number of states as failed, failing, or "causes for concern" and suggests that the United States follow a policy of "early and aggressive" intervention in those nations. Her rationalization is that without early intervention such states act as hosts to terrorist groups, trigger regional conflagrations, and ultimately require far greater resources in terms of conflict resolution and peacekeeping. However, many of the nations that Rice characterizes as either failed or failing—such as Somalia, Sierra Leone, and Cote D'Ivoire—do not serve as significant hosts of terrorist groups. On the other hand, terrorist groups such as the Irish Republican Army and the Basque separatists have operated for years in the United Kingdom and Spain, two nations that can hardly be considered candidates for nation building.

Economic freedom, respect for private enterprise and entrepreneurship, and the rule of law are the key elements of growth and prosperity.

Rice also fails to consider that foreign intervention often has unintended consequences, and may even result in wider regional conflict, as happened in Afghanistan itself during the 1980s, or in Southeast Asia in the 1960s. She does consider the costs of exacerbated regional tensions and weapons proliferation that could be incurred by the United States if it doesn't preempt state failure, but she ignores the cumulative cost to the United States of "early and aggressive" intervention in what may amount to dozens of countries around the world. Such a policy is questionable in any era, but it is especially so today, when American military forces are already strained to the breaking point as they police the sprawling American empire. More importantly, the tremendous drain on resources from nation-building exercises provides little value to national security, a security that appears shakier today, following the events of September 11, than it did at the end of the Cold War.

Rice is not alone in her calls for preemptive nation building. In 2002, Sen. Chuck Hagel sponsored a $3.3 billion program for economic, political, humanitarian, and security assistance for Afghanistan over four years. Less than three months after President Bush signed the aid package into law, Hagel was back for more, calling for still more money for Afghanistan to create stability and prosperity. Sen. Barbara Boxer is even more ambitious, calling for the expansion of International Security Assistance Force operations to areas outside Kabul because "women face harsh restrictions under local leaders." Such calls ignore prior lessons in Afghanistan, where the imposition of a foreign ideology by the Soviets only served to deepen resentment by locals who then focused their attention on hastening the end of the foreign occupation.

Sen. Joseph Biden has been one of the most vocal supporters of nation building in Afghanistan, calling for an Afghan Marshall Plan [Europe's post–World War II recovery plan]. However, the Marshall Plan analogy for Afghanistan is inappropriate. Local conditions contributed more to Europe's recovery from the Second World War than did Marshall Plan aid. The total amount of aid never amounted to more than 5 percent of GNP [gross national product] in the Marshall Plan countries, and there is no data to suggest that this aid was instrumental; Belgium's post-war recovery was the fastest in Europe even though the Belgians received a relatively small share of Marshall Plan money; the British, on the other hand, received the most aid, but had the slowest rate of economic growth in post-war Europe. Economic freedom, respect for private enterprise and entrepreneurship, and the rule of law are the key elements of growth and prosperity. Foreign aid is often counterproductive to these ends.

Simply put, there does not appear to be a positive correlation between the extent of economic and political intervention and the ability of outside forces to shape a nation's destiny. The Council of Foreign Relations–Asia Society task force report recommends increased U.S. intervention in the Karzai-warlord disputes and an enlarged role in Afghanistan's reconstruction, ostensibly to prevent the nation from slipping back into anarchy and again becoming a terrorist haven. But the longer the United States and other foreign governments remain in Afghanistan, the greater the likelihood that their efforts—notwithstanding their noble intentions—will be seen as an attempt to subvert the will of the Afghan people. An extended American presence, therefore, will create an atmosphere conducive to supporting the very terrorist elements that presence is intended to eliminate.

Security Before Reconstruction

Afghanistan was freed from Taliban rule. Since then [in December 2001], attacks by Taliban loyalists, al Qaeda remnants, and renegade warlords have undermined fledgling reconstruction efforts in the nation and exposed the Karzai regime's lack of control outside Kabul. Karzai has pressed the Bush administration for an expanded commitment to the rebuilding of Afghanistan, and many observers, including some in the U.S. Congress, have seconded his calls.

However, a number of factors in Afghanistan, and past experiences in nation-building exercises around the world, suggest that pumping resources and effort into reconstruction in the absence of security and economic order will not have the desired outcome. An increased U.S. commitment to civilian reconstruction may only distract us from the goal of eliminating anti-U.S. Islamic extremists who will sabotage any rebuilding efforts. Although much of the focus to date has been on empowering a strong central government in Afghanistan, deep ethnic fissures and the persistent strength of the regional warlords suggest that such an aim is too ambitious.

Pumping resources and effort into reconstruction in the absence of security and economic order will not have the desired outcome.

The U.S. military forces currently operating in Afghanistan should concentrate on smashing the Taliban and al Qaeda remnants who are regrouping along the Afghanistan-Pakistan border. Once this goal is achieved, U.S. forces need not remain in the nation. Following the end of military operations, the focus could then shift to monitoring Afghanistan and its neighbors to ensure that forces that threaten the United States are not resurrected. Most of this work can be conducted by U.S. intelligence services in cooperation with our allies in the region.

"The United States abandoned Afghanistan after the Cold War," was a common refrain heard after the September 11 attacks. Indeed, the national security threat that was incubating in Afghanistan since the mid-1990s was ignored at a grave cost. A preemptive move against al Qaeda and the Taliban, and their allies, might have headed off the threat that culminated in 9-11. However, it is far from clear that sustained nation building by the United States after the Soviet withdrawal would have been successful in the 1990s or would even be feasible today.

In the aftermath of the disastrous Soviet attempt at nation building in Afghanistan, any peace enforced at the point of the gun would have served to turn many of the mujahadeen factions against the United States. The U.S. military would have had to take sides in the competition among the irregular forces led by the likes of Burnahuddin Rabbani, Ahmed Shah Masood, Rashid Dostum, Golbuddin Hekmatyar, and Ismail Khan. A similar attempt to interpose American troops between competing warlords following a Soviet withdrawal from an impoverished country met with an unfortunate and embarrassing end, and the situation in Afghanistan is far worse than the one encountered in Somalia in 1993. Furthermore, given the intense rivalry among neighboring powers over influence in Afghanistan, a long-term military presence could well have enmeshed the United States in regional quagmires such as the India-Pakistan conflict and confrontation with Iran. Instead of recrimination, instead of replaying the errors of the past, U.S. policy toward Afghanistan in the 21st century should focus on the known threats that still operate there.

Lessons from prior experiences in nation building can be applied beyond Afghanistan to a broader policy framework. A blanket policy of early and aggressive intervention in overseas hotspots is likely to be counterproductive and costly. Although the United States cannot afford to ignore national security threats in the post 9-11 era, neither can it afford to get entangled in the innumerable conflicts and tensions around the globe, risking distractions from the crucial goals of hunting and eliminating America's enemies.

3

Increased Taliban Attacks Pose Challenges to Reconstruction Efforts

Sankar Sen

As the date of the first free elections in Afghanistan in decades approached at the end of 2004, the Taliban determination to thwart the efforts of the U.S.-backed Afghan provisional government increased. In the following selection, the former director-general of India's National Human Rights Commission, Sankar Sen, contends that a lack of international commitment of troops threatens Afghan security in general and the elections specifically. He also describes the continued threat posed by local militias not loyal to Afghan president Hamid Karzai's central government. If the United States and the coalition forces do not fully commit to stabilizing the situation in Afghanistan, Sen argues, the Taliban will disrupt the elections and eventually could once again take over the country.

After the end of the war bringing down the brutal Taliban regime in Afghanistan, [British prime minister] Tony Blair had said in November 2000 that in rebuilding their country, the people of Afghanistan would receive the full support of the coalition. "We must give you all help and support that you need", he said, "and that support will be forthcoming". But Afghanistan remains a trouble-torn country even three years after liberation. Peace and stability have eluded its people. More than 800 people have been killed in [2004] in a wave of violence unleashed mostly by the remnants of the Taliban who are opposed to "Karzai's US-backed government".

Lack of International Support

The Afghans have done their bit in setting up an interim government and holding a Loya Jirga or Grand Council to set up a legitimate administration. They have drafted a constitution and are preparing to hold a democratic presidential and parliamentary election. Western powers, however, have not fulfilled their commitment. Disorder and violence stalk the land, particularly in southern and eastern parts of Afghanistan. The Taliban is down but not out. They have vowed to disrupt the October [2004] elections and have carried out a string of attacks killing civilians, government employees and election workers. Recently there was an explosion in the city of Herat killing five people and wounding 34. The Governor of Herat Ismail Khan is a warlord with his own militiamen.

Efforts of the central government to disarm rogue private militias have not been so far successful.

Efforts of the central government to disarm rogue private militias have not been so far successful. Disarming thousands of irregular fighters under the command of regional warlords is the key to Afghanistan's stability. President Hamid Karzai told the *New York Times* that Afghanistan's private militia was a greater threat than the Islamic militants of Taliban. According to him, only 10,000 of an estimated 50,000 militias could be demobilised and that is why the parliamentary elections had to be postponed till April [2004]. More forceful measures are necessary to deal with militias who have often defied Kabul's orders and added to Afghanistan's instability. It is true there are about 20,000 coalition troops, mostly Americans, in Afghanistan but they are mainly to hunt down Osama bin Laden and other remnants of Al-Qaida. American forces during their operations are resorting to search and destroy missions and revenge killings. This has further alienated the civilian population. Violation of human rights by the American troops in their operations in Afghanistan has been documented and indicted by the Human Rights Watch in its report.

Elections have already been put back from the target date and the delay in holding the election will fulfill the plans of the Taliban.

The task of providing basic internal security has been given to International Security Assistance Force (ISAF) comprising troops provided by NATO powers. But their number is totally inadequate. They have a total strength of 6,500 men and they are mainly based in [the capital city of] Kabul. In consequence, the Afghan capital is safe but not the rest of the country. This indeed marks a serious failure of NATO. The organisation has been asked to run ISAF and extend its remit outside the capital. But so far its success has been limited. Warlords and drug barons rule most of the country and anyone who opposes them is threatened with death.

Challenges for Security Forces

NATO's European peace-keepers promised to restore peace in the country ahead of the election but have so far singularly failed to do so. Terrorist violence sweeps the land. A number of workers of different aid agencies as well as election workers have been killed. In [the Afghan city of] Mazar-e-Sharif warlords like Rashid Dostam and Attah Mohammad are fighting their battles. Elections have already been put back from the target date and the delay in holding the election will fulfil the plans of the Taliban. [As of August 2004] only around 3.5 million of Afghanistan's estimated 10 million eligible voters, mostly in and around major cities, have been registered as voters, if Hamid Karzai whom the United States is backing is elected on a narrow franchise the legitimacy of his government will be compromised.

ISAF recently decided to post regional garrisons known as Provincial Reconstruction Teams (PRT) throughout Northern and Western Afghanistan on the eve of the election. American-led coalition forces will perform policing in the more volatile South and East Afghanistan. At the recently held summit in Istanbul, NATO members came to an agreement to make sure that successful elections are held in Afghanistan and the country does not drift into total chaos. Alliance partners decided to raise the number of troops from 6,500 to 8,000. This is a small number compared to 60,000 American, British and French troops sent to Bosnia to bring peace there. Further, NATO is divided on this issue. France is resisting the plea for more NATO troops made by President Hamid Karzai. Afghanistan is thus being asked to fend for itself. The composition of ISAF forces shows that most of the NATO countries are dragging their feet and avoiding despatch of more troops. Germany and Canada have provided the bulk of the forces; other countries are unwilling to contribute men and money for a land which they fear may slip back to chaos and become a failed State. Many NATO countries also feel they are not bound to fulfil NATO's peace-keeping duties [because] the Cold War is over. ISAF commanders are also hamstrung by the restrictions imposed by their governments. For example, German soldiers that are keeping peace in Kunduz are constitutionally barred from performing riot control duties.

Taliban Determined to Disrupt

According to the existing arrangements, Germany will contribute a garrison to remote Faizabad and a British-run coalition PRT in Mazar-e-Sharif will come under ISAF's command. The Netherlands will open a new PRT in northern Baghlan province and Turkey will provide a force for another PRT. These small measures are unlikely to bring peace to an increasingly dangerous land. The overall effect is going to be slim. Afghanistan has provided NATO an opportunity to show its usefulness in the post–Cold War world. It should redeem itself and not allow this opportunity to slip by.

US forces in Afghanistan have now begun a military operation called "Operation Lighting Resort" aimed at providing security for the October [2004] presidential election. The purpose of the operation, according to Pentagon, is to ensure the security of the electoral process. These operations are being launched jointly with the Afghan national army and the police. A large number of US troops are participating in it.

The Taliban has vowed to disrupt the election process and will leave no stone unturned to achieve their goals. Any delay in holding presidential and parliamentary elections would mark a victory for them. However, for the success of the election and subsequent formation of a representative government, peace and security are essential. Otherwise, the new constitution would suffer the same fate as the country's previous ones which were largely undermined by facts on the ground. There is also popular apprehension that the Americans might at some time cut their losses and seek an exit strategy. The Taliban estimates that time is in their favour.

Chronology

329–327 B.C.
Alexander the Great conquers the region that will later become Afghanistan.

7th–18th Centuries
Muslim conquest; various Islamic rulers vie for control.

1747–1818
The Durrani Dynasty unites most of the region.

1826–1863
Emir Dost Mohammad reigns.

1838–1842
The First Afghan War is waged between the British and the Afghans.

1878
The Second Afghan War takes place.

1893
The Durand Agreement establishes the modern-day borders of Afghanistan.

1907
The British guarantee Afghan independence but maintain control of foreign affairs.

1919
The Third Afghan War ends in complete independence for Afghanistan.

1933–1973
King Mohammad Zahir Shah rules the country, first under the guidance of relatives and then, after 1963, on his own.

1964
Afghanistan's first constitution rules that women and men are legally equal. This and other liberal dictates in the document anger rural Afghans and create political problems.

1973
King Zahir Shah is overthrown in a military coup.

1978
The People's Democratic Party of Afghanistan takes over the country in a military coup.

1979
The USSR invades Afghanistan and takes over the government.

1987–1988
The Soviets withdraw from Afghanistan and install Mohammad Najibullah as president.

1987–1992
A civil war between warring mujahideens rages.

1992
President Najibullah's government collapses.

1992–1994
Mujahideen are the official government of Afghanistan.

1994
November: The Taliban captures Kandahar.

1995
September: The Taliban captures Herat. The Taliban bans the education of women.

1996
September: The Taliban captures Jalalabad and Kabul, causing ten thousand people to leave Jalalabad for Pakistan. The USSR takes an official position against the Taliban.
October: The Taliban takes Badghis Province. The United Nations asks all countries to oppose the Taliban because of its poor treatment of women. Fifty thousand people leave Kabul for Pakistan.

1997
May: The Taliban fails in an attempt to take over Mazar-e Sharif. Two hundred thousand people flee to Kabul after having been evacuated from their homes in northern Afghanistan. The Voice of Sharia, the Taliban-run radio station, broadcasts a defense of the Taliban's treatment of the Afghan people.

July: An oil pipeline construction agreement is signed between Pakistan, Turkmenistan, Delta Oil of Saudi Arabia, and UNOCAL of the United States.

1998

August: The Taliban captures Mazar-e Sharif. The United States bombs targets in Afghanistan, believing Osama bin Laden, the leader of the terrorist group al Qaeda, who had official asylum there, was responsible for attacks on U.S. embassies in the Middle East.

1999

The UN Security Council imposes sanctions on the Taliban.

2000

September: The Taliban captures Taliqan in the northeast. About 170,000 people leave Taliqan for Pakistan; 80,000 more are displaced but remain in Afghanistan.
December: The UN Security Council imposes more sanctions on the Taliban.

2001

September 11: Terrorists attack the World Trade Center and the Pentagon. The United States believes Osama bin Laden is behind the attacks.
October 7: After the Taliban refuses to turn Bin Laden over to the United States, the United States begins bombing strategic Taliban sites in Afghanistan. Bin Laden issues a statement calling on all Muslims to wage a holy war against America. Pro-Taliban, anti-U.S. demonstrations erupt in Pakistan.
October 19: The United States begins ground assaults against the Taliban with the aid of Afghan resistance fighters known as the Northern Alliance.
October 26: The Taliban executes former mujahideen leader Abdul Haq, his nephew, and anti-Taliban commander Haji Dawran for treason and espionage.
November 10: The Northern Alliance forces take cities of Mazar-e Sharif and Taliqan from the Taliban.
November 11: Several international journalists are killed in a Taliban ambush.
November 12: The Northern Alliance captures Herat and moves on Kabul.
November 13: The Northern Alliance seizes Kabul. The Taliban retreats from Kandahar.

November 15: The Taliban leaves Kandahar.

November 21: Taliban commanders in Kunduz meet with Northern Alliance leaders to negotiate a surrender. The Taliban claims to still control the provinces of Kandahar, Helmand, Uruzgan, Zabol, and part of Ghazni Province. The Taliban claims not to know the whereabouts of Osama bin Laden.

November 24: The Taliban surrenders Kunduz.

November 25: Hundreds of U.S. Marines land near Kandahar to fight Taliban and al Qaeda on the ground.

November 27: Afghan leaders meet with UN representatives in Bonn, Germany, to work out guidelines for a post-Taliban government.

November 29: The United States continues air strikes on Kandahar. Mullah Omar, the top Taliban leader, urges Taliban forces to keep fighting.

December 5: Hamid Karzai is selected as interim leader of Afghanistan by delegates in Bonn.

December 7: The Taliban surrenders Kandahar and withdraws from the city. Former Taliban soldiers infiltrate nearby villages and continue to enforce Taliban rules.

December 11: Bin Laden and his men retreat to mountains near Tora Bora in eastern Afghanistan. The United States bombs a complex of caves in the hopes of killing Bin Laden.

December 16: The United States declares that al Qaeda has been removed from Afghanistan. The U.S. embassy in Kabul reopens.

December 20: Afghan officials agree to the presence of a UN peacekeeping force in the hopes of rebuilding Afghanistan.

December 22: Hamid Karzai is sworn in as chairman of an interim government. The United States officially recognizes the Afghan government for the first time since 1979.

December 26: U.S. forces continue to hunt for Bin Laden near Tora Bora.

2002

January: The Taliban admits defeat. Seven top Taliban officials who surrendered at Kandahar are released, and it is assumed that they leave the country.

February: The United States continues to bomb Taliban and al Qaeda sites and search for Mullah Omar and Osama bin Laden. Taliban and al Qaeda prisoners of war are imprisoned at the U.S. naval station at Guantánamo Bay in Cuba.

March: The United States begins Operation Anaconda, in which U.S. and Afghan soldiers try to force the remaining Taliban and al Qaeda fighters from the country.

April: Former king Zahir Shah returns but makes no claim on the throne.

May: Allied forces continue their military campaign to route remaining soldiers of al Qaeda and the Taliban from the southeast.

June 11: The *loya jirga*, or grand council, opens.

June 13: The *loya jirga* elects Karzai as interim head of state. Karzai selects members of his administration, which is to serve until 2004.

July: Vice President Haji Abdul Qadir is assassinated by gunmen in Kabul. A U.S. air raid in Uruzgan Province kills forty-eight civilians, many of them members of a wedding party.

September: Hamid Karzai is nearly assassinated by a Taliban assassin.

October: The top UN envoy in Afghanistan tells the UN Security Council that the new Afghan government headed by Karzai does not have the power to deal with the underlying problems that cause security threats in the country.

November: Rival factions in northern Afghanistan begin turning in their weapons as part of a UN program to curb violence. Former king Zahir Shah inaugurates a special committee to draft a new constitution for the country.

December: Afghan commander Amanullah Khan launches an attack on positions held by Ismail Khan, governor of Herat Province.

2003

January: The Afghan security chief claims that minor clashes have been reported between Afghan forces and suspected members of the Taliban. Karzai announces the formation of four commissions to accelerate the disarmament of warlord armies and to rebuild the Afghan National Army.

February: President Karzai visits the U.S. Senate Foreign Relations Committee in Washington, D.C. In the hearing, Karzai gives an optimistic view of the state of Afghanistan and disputes claims that one hundred thousand militiamen living in the provinces are beyond the control of his government. Factional fighting flares up between rival Afghan groups within seven hundred yards of the perimeter of Bagram Air Base.

March: The first foreign aid worker is killed in Afghanistan since the Taliban was removed from power. There is a surge of attacks against U.S. troops in southern Afghanistan. The United States launches Operation Valiant Strike in Kandahar, the largest U.S. mission in Afghanistan since Operation Anaconda. Afghan authorities raid a house in Kandahar and arrest ten former Taliban members. Police seize arms, explosives, and land mines. The first Afghan radio station programmed solely for women begins broadcasting in Kabul.

April: Officials announce a UN program to disarm, demobilize, and reintegrate an estimated one hundred thousand fighters across Afghanistan in the next three years. Nearly fifty suspected Taliban fighters attack a checkpoint in the Shingai district of Zabul Province; the fighters flee after a brief battle.

May: Defense Secretary Donald Rumsfeld declares that Afghanistan is now secure, despite evidence that pro-Taliban soldiers continue to attack government buildings, U.S. bases, and aid workers on a daily basis. Afghanistan's membership in the International Criminal Court (ICC) takes effect. The ICC will have the authority to investigate and prosecute serious war crimes and crimes against humanity committed on Afghan soil.

June: Clashes in Kandahar between Taliban loyalists and government forces leave forty-nine people dead.

August: NATO assumes charge of security in Kabul.

September: U.S.-led forces fight back a group of Taliban rebels.

December: The U.S. military begins Operation Avalanche, which involves some two thousand soldiers.

2004

January: At the *loya jirga*, leaders adopt a new constitution with provisions for a strong centralized government and presidency.

February: Taliban leader Mullah Dadullah warns Afghan citizens not to vote in the presidential elections scheduled for June.

March: President Karzai announces that Afghanistan's first post-Taliban elections will be postponed until September. The Taliban vows to disrupt the process.

June: Fearing for the safety of its workers, Doctors Without Borders suspends its work in Afghanistan.

July: President Karzai pushes the presidential election to October 2004 and in a surprise move, chooses a new running mate, Ahmad Zia Massood.

October 9: Presidential elections are held in Afghanistan.

November 3: The United Nations–Afghan joint electoral commission announces that interim leader Hamid Karzai is the winner of the October 9 presidential election.

For Further Research

Books

Asad AbuKhalil, *Bin Laden, Islam, and America's New "War On Terror."* New York: Seven Stories, 2002.

George Arney, *Afghanistan.* London: Mandarin, 1990.

Anthony Arnold, *The Fateful Pebble: Afghanistan's Role in the Fall of the Soviet Empire.* Novato, CA: Presidio, 1993.

G.D. Bakshi, *The First Faultline War.* New Delhi: Lancer, 2002.

Susan Barakat, ed., *Reconstructing War-Torn Societies: Afghanistan.* New York: Palgrave Macmillan, 2004.

Robert F. Baumann, *Russian-Soviet Unconventional Wars in the Caucasus, Central Asia, and Afghanistan.* Ft. Leavenworth: U.S. Army Command and General Staff College, 1993.

Gary K. Bertsch, Cassady B. Craft, and Scott A. Jones, eds., *Crossroads and Conflict: Security and Foreign Policy in the Caucasus and Central Asia.* New York: Routledge, 1999.

Stephen Biddle, *Afghanistan and the Future of Warfare.* Carlisle Barracks, PA: Strategic Studies Institute, U.S. Army War College, 2002.

Yossef Bodansky, *Bin Laden: The Man Who Declared War on America.* Rocklin, CA: Prima, 1999.

John K. Cooley, *Unholy Wars: Afghanistan, American, and International Terrorism.* Sterling, VA: Pluto, 2002.

Diego Cordovez, *Out of Afghanistan: The Inside Story of the Soviet Withdrawal.* New York: Oxford University Press, 1995.

David B. Edwards, *Heroes of the Age: Moral Fault Lines on the Afghan Frontier.* Berkeley: University of California Press, 1996.

Anoushiravan Ehteshami, ed., *From the Gulf to Central Asia: Players in the New Great Game.* Exeter, UK: University of Exeter Press, 1995.

Martin Ewans, *Afghanistan: A New History*. Surrey, UK: Curzon, 2002.

———, *Afghanistan: A Short History of Its People and Politics*. New York: Perennial, 2002.

Mark Galeotti, *Afghanistan: The Soviet Union's Last War*. London: Frank Cass, 1995.

Mir Gholam Mohammad Ghobar, *Afghanistan in the Course of History*. Vol. 2. Trans. Sherief A. Fayez. Alexandria, VA: Hashmat K. Gobar, 2001.

M.J. Gohari, *Taliban: Ascent to Power*. Oxford: Oxford University Press, 2001.

Larry P. Goodson, *Afghanistan's Endless War: State Failure, Regional Politics, and the Rise of the Taliban*. Seattle: University of Washington Press, 2001.

Michael Griffin, *Reaping the Whirlwind: The Taliban Movement in Afghanistan*. London: Pluto, 2003.

David C. Isby, *War in a Distant Country: Afghanistan, Invasion, and Resistance*. London: Arms and Armour, 1989.

Ali Ahmad Jalali and Lester W. Grau, *Afghan Guerrilla Warfare: In the Words of the Mujahideen Fighters*. St. Paul, MN: MBI, 2001.

Tom Lansford, *A Bitter Harvest: U.S. Foreign Policy and Afghanistan*. Burlington, VT: Ashgate, 2003.

Ralph Magnus and Eden Naby, *Afghanistan, Mullah, Marx, and Mujahid*. India: HarperCollins, 1998.

William Maley, *The Afghan Wars*. New York: Palgrave Macmillan, 2002.

William Maley, ed., *Fundamentalism Reborn? Afghanistan and the Taliban*. London: C. Hurst, 1998.

Peter Marsden, *The Taliban: War and Religion in Afghanistan*. London: Zed, 2002.

Kamal Matinnudin, *The Taliban Phenomenon: Afghanistan, 1994–1997*. Oxford: Oxford University Press, 1999.

Amalendu Misra, *Afghanistan: The Labyrinth of Violence*. Malden, MA: Polity, 2004.

Neamatollah Nojumi, *The Rise of the Taliban in Afghanistan: Mass Mobilization, Civil War, and the Future of the Region*. New York: Palgrave, 2002.

Asta Olsen, *Islam and Politics in Afghanistan*. London: Curzon, 1995.

Hooman Peimani, *Regional Security and the Future of Central Asia*. New York: Praeger, 1998.

Rasul Bakhsh Rais, *War Without Winners: Afghanistan's Uncertain Transition After the Cold War*. Oxford: Oxford University Press, 1994.

Ahmed Rashid, *Jihad: The Rise of Militant Islam in Central Asia*. New York: Penguin, 2002.

———, *Taliban: Militant Islam, Oil, and Fundamentalism in Central Asia*. New Haven, CT: Yale University Press, 1998.

Jeffrey J. Roberts, *The Origins of Conflict in Afghanistan*. Westport, CT: Praeger, 2003.

Olivier Roy, *Afghanistan, from Holy War to Civil War*. Princeton, NJ: Princeton University Press, 1995.

Barnett Rubin, *The Fragmentation of Afghanistan: State Formation and Collapse in the International System*. New Haven, CT: Yale University Press, 2002.

———, *The Search for Peace in Afghanistan: From Buffer State to Failed State*. New Haven, CT: Yale University Press, 1995.

Boris Z. Rumer, *Central Asia and the New Global Economy*. Armonk, NY: M.E. Sharpe, 2000.

Roald Sagdeev and Susan Eisenhower, eds., *Islam and Central Asia: An Enduring Legacy or an Evolving Threat?* New York: Center for Political Studies, 2000.

Shaul Shay, *The Endless Jihad: The Mujahhidin, the Taliban and Bin Laden*. Herzliyya, Israel: International Policy Institute for Counter-Terrorism, 2002.

Rosemarie Skaine, *The Women of Afghanistan Under the Taliban*. Jefferson, NC: McFarland, November 2001.

Stephen Tanner, *Afghanistan: A Military History from Alexander the Great to the Fall of the Taliban*. New York: Da Capo, 2002.

Robert S. Tripp, *Supporting Air and Space Expeditionary Forces: Lessons from Operation Enduring Freedom*. Santa Monica, CA: RAND, 2004.

Mark Urban, *War in Afghanistan*. New York: St. Martin's, 1988.

Periodicals

Benazir Bhutto, "Pakistan's Dilemma," *Harvard International Review*, Spring 2002.

Jason Burke and Peter Beaumont, "West Pays Warlords to Stay in Line," *Guardian*, July 21, 2002.

Bruce Crumley et al., "Hate Club," *Time*, November 12, 2001.

Laura Flanders, "Afghan Feminists Speak Out," *Progressive*, November 2001.

Carlotta Gall, "Expecting Taliban, but Finding Only Horror," *New York Times*, July 8, 2002.

Michael Ignatieff, "Nation-Building Lite," *New York Times Magazine*, July 28, 2002.

Mark Kaufman, "U.S. Lands in Middle of Afghan Feuding," *Washington Post*, March 28, 2003.

Elie D. Krakowski, "How to Win the Peace in Afghanistan," *Weekly Standard*, July 8, 2002.

Rose V. Lindgren, "When Foreign Intervention Is Justified: Women Under the Taliban," *Humanist*, July/August 2002.

Michael Massing, "Losing the Peace?" *Nation*, May 13, 2002.

Tim McGirk, "Al Qaeda's New Hideouts," *Time*, July 29, 2002.

Rod Nordland, Sami Yousafzai, and Babak Dehghanpishheh, "How al Qaeda Slipped Away," *Newsweek*, August 19, 2002.

Hooman Peiami, "Afghanistan-Based International Drug Trafficking: An International Threat," *Central Asia-Caucasus Analyst*, May 8, 2002.

Olivier Roy, "Why War Is Going On in Afghanistan: The Afghan Crisis in Perspective," *Journal of International Affairs*, December 2000–February 2001.

Horst Rutsch, "Afghanistan: On the Road to Recovery," *UN Chronicle*, March–May 2002.

Philip Smucker, "Afghans Put Off Key Decisions," *Christian Science Monitor*, June 18, 2002.

S. Frederick Starr, "A Sweet Sixteen: Plenty of Reasons to Cheer the Post-Taliban Afghanistan," *National Review*, August 11, 2003.

Jessica Stern, "The Protean Enemy," *Foreign Affairs*, July/ August 2003.

Raymond Whittaker, "Behind the Burqa: Women Who Fight the Taliban," *In These Times*, November 12, 2001.

Web Sites

About Afghanistan, www.aboutafghanistan.com. This search engine directs researchers to a wide variety of resources on the Web that track topics related to Afghanistan.

Afghan Online Press, www.aopnews.com. This Web site is a media center for current events in Afghanistan that combines radio and television news broadcasts with printed articles in a variety of languages.

Human Rights Watch: Afghanistan, www.hrw.org/campaigns/afghanistan. Human Rights Watch is an independent, nongovernmental organization dedicated to protecting the rights of people around the world.

The Islamic Transitional State of Afghanistan, www.afghanistangov.org. This is the central Web site of the Islamic Transitional State of Afghanistan. It provides information on Afghanistan's national budget, the government's donor assistance database, and on major international conferences on Afghanistan's reconstruction.

The Reconstruction of Afghanistan, www.developmentgateway.org/node/13411. The Development Gateway is an interactive portal for information and knowledge sharing on sustainable development and poverty reduction. This site is dedicated to the reconstruction of Afghanistan.

The Revolutionary Association of the Women of Afghanistan, www.rawa.org. RAWA, the Revolutionary Association of the Women of Afghanistan, was established in Kabul, Afghanistan, in 1977 as an independent political/ social organization of women fighting for human rights and for social justice in Afghanistan. This site tracks developments in Afghanistan from a social justice perspective.

Index